Benedicamus Domino!
Let us Bless the Lord!

The Theological Foundations of the Liturgical Renewal

Benedicamus Domino!
Let us Bless the Lord!

The Theological Foundations of the Liturgical Renewal

Attila Miklósházy, S.J.

NOVALIS

© 2001 Novalis, Saint Paul University, Ottawa, Canada

Cover design and layout: Caroline Gagnon
Editor: Bernadette Gasslein

Business Office:
Novalis
49 Front Street East, 2nd Floor
Toronto, Ontario, Canada
M5E 1B3

Phone: 1-800-387-7164 or (416) 363-3303
Fax: 1-800-204-4140 or (416) 363-9409
E-mail: novalis@interlog.com

National Library of Canada Cataloguing in Publication Data

Mikloshazy, Attila

    Benedicamus Domino! = Let us bless the Lord! : the theological foundations of the liturgical renewal

ISBN 2-89507-234-5

    1. Catholic Church—Liturgy. 2. Catholic Church—Doctrines. 3. Liturgical movement—Catholic Church. I. Title. II. Title: Let us bless the Lord!

BX1975.M53 2002   264'.02   C2001-903380-X

Printed in Canada.

All rights reserved. No part of this publication may be reproduced, stored in a retrieval system, or transmitted in any form, or by any means, electronic, mechanical, photocopying, recording, or otherwise, without the written permission of the publisher.

We acknowledge the financial support of the Government of Canada through the Book Publishing Industry Development Program (BPIDP) for our publishing activities.

Nihil Obstat: Rev. Msgr. John K. Murphy, P.H.
Censor Deputatus
Toronto, October 17, 2000

Imprimatur: Aloysius Cardinal Ambrozic
Archiepiscopus Torontinus
Toronto, October 17, 2000

The Nihil Obstat and Imprimatur are official declarations that a book or pamphlet is free of doctrinal or moral error. No implication is contained therein that those who have granted the Nihil Obstat and Imprimatur agree with the contents, opinions or statements expressed.

Contents

Preface 9
1. The Historical Background of Liturgical Renewal 11

I. Theological Principles of the Liturgy

2. Liturgy: An Encounter with the Sacred 21
3. Liturgy: Acknowledgement of the Creator and Covenant God ... 29
4. Liturgy: The Exercise of the Priesthood of Christ 39
5. Liturgy: The Privileged Place of the Working of the Holy Spirit.. 49
6. Liturgy: The Public Worship of the Whole Church 55
7. Liturgy: Performed in the World of Symbols 65
8. Liturgy: Dialogue in Words 69
9. Liturgy: A Process in Three Phases 81

II. Liturgy of the Sacraments

10. The Liturgy of Christian Initiation 89
11. The Liturgy of the Eucharist 103
12. The Liturgy of Forgiveness and Reconciliation 123
13. The Liturgy of the Anointing of the Sick 133
14. The Liturgy of Marriage 141
15. The Liturgy of Ordination 145

Appendix: Some Forgotten Truths About the Priesthood 149

Preface

The origin of this book goes back to my many years of teaching liturgy to seminarians and university students, and giving lectures and workshops to priests and lay people around the country. The aim of these lectures was primarily to promote liturgical renewal by emphasizing the theological foundations of the liturgical reform, and, especially, by imbuing it with the true spirit of the liturgy. Because of this practical aim, I have omitted footnotes that I might have provided to a more academic audience.

The content of this book can be divided into two main parts. After a brief historical overview of the liturgical movement, the first part explores the theological principles of liturgy by simply answering the question: What is liturgy? I give eight partial descriptions of the liturgy. All must be considered together for an adequate understanding of the liturgy.

In the second part of the book I consider the liturgies of the seven sacraments, and offer some practical comments in light of the revised liturgical rites, and the principles articulated in Part I.

May these reflections deepen our knowledge of the liturgy and help us produce a true liturgical spirituality for a better celebration.

Attila Miklósházy, S.J.
Toronto
November 2001

Chapter 1

The Historical Background of Liturgical Renewal

The Second Vatican Council is a milestone in the history of liturgy. After the Council of Trent, the liturgy was influenced by the Baroque spirit and by Romanticism until Pope Pius X started to renew it at the beginning of the 20th century. "To renew all things in Christ!" (*Instaurare omnia in Christo!*) was his motto. His decrees planted in the hearts of many people the seeds of the awareness that, because here God speaks to human hearts, we can do much in the Church through the liturgy. Although we need certain structures and organizations to assure good liturgy, the decisive factor is liturgical spirituality, which Pius X, and later, Dom Lambert Beauduin and many others tried to emphasize in the first half of the twentieth century.

Much had also been done in the field of liturgical scholarship. Its leaders included the Benedictine monks of Maria Laach, Dom Odo Casel and Dom Herbert Herwegen; the Jesuit theologians of Innsbruck, Hugo and Karl Rahner, and especially Joseph Andreas Jungmann. Singled out among the French is Louis Bouyer. In England, the Anglican Benedictine Dom Gregory Dix laid down the scientific foundations of modern liturgical scholarship. Alongside the growing insights in liturgy we also notice the development of sacramental theology, especially after World War II. Odo Casel's "Mystery-presence" *(Mysteriengegenwart)* revolutionized liturgical theology so much that today even Protestant theologians accept his thesis. Perhaps we find the greatest *rapprochement* among the Christian churches in this area. We should also mention the Dominican Edward Schillebeeckx, whose book on sacramental theology, *Christ, the Sacrament of the Encounter with God*, significantly influenced our understanding of liturgy. Then Karl Rahner's *The Church and the Sacraments* further directed our attention to the ecclesial dimensions of the liturgy.

The work of these famous, brilliant and pastorally sensitive theologians, along with that of others before the Second Vatican Council, had prepared well, and well supported with historical, theological and pastoral arguments the first document of the Council, the *Constitution on the Sacred Liturgy (Sacrosanctum Concilium)*. It laid down the theological foundations of our liturgy. The Council thus finished the work of the twentieth century liturgical movement which had begun with Pius X. This movement was not a neatly organized project; rather, it progressed by virtue of the benevolent enthusiasm of many people and the support of the occasional papal endorsement (such as Pius XII's *Mediator Dei*), until it arrived at the Council. Now we have the first liturgical constitution in the history of the Church, upon which we can build a solid liturgical spirituality.

What happened after the Council? From 1963-1978 two different developments emerged. The Council directed, first of all, that the liturgical forms (books, rites) were to be reformed. The executors of this official liturgical reform were the same experts who up to now had led the liturgical movement. In 15 years, more or less, this liturgical reform, the initial revision of liturgical books and rites, was completed. This revision was necessary because it became evident that the renewed theology of the liturgy required new forms. These new forms were constructed according to well-grounded theological, historical and liturgical principles, after widespread pastoral consultation by the liturgical experts themselves. Their work gave us the revised liturgical books, a veritable treasure for the Church. Still, this was not enough.

The life of the Church manifests itself most clearly in the liturgy. If there is any problem in the Church, we sense it right away in the liturgy. And problems emerge nowadays both in society and in the Church. For instance, the problem of freedom emerged after Vatican II. No doubt, both World Wars contributed to the fact that people feared any prescribed forms and social obligations imposed by some authority. A certain critical urge emerged, in which some people began to criticize and judge everyone and everything. The progress of science may also have contributed to this attitude; because of the achievements of science some human beings think they can do everything by their own power. The documents of Vatican II, such as *Gaudium et Spes*, emphasize openness to, and dialogue with, the world. Consequently, the Church paid more attention to social problems than before. Thus, the main mission of the Church was considered to be service *(diakonia)* to the world. Likewise, the emphasis on the dignity of the human person is an idea that arises from the conciliar documents. Certain risks are always inherent in the application of these excellent Christian principles. The dangers we face elsewhere we must also face in the liturgy: changing attitudes to and patterns of acceptance of authority, service to the world becoming secularism instead of secularization. We must also face these tendencies in the liturgy.

During the 15 years just after the Council, while the experts and liturgists were occupied with the revision of the liturgical books, a certain liturgical revolution broke out. The Council had awakened in many people the desire to do something, to produce something new—as soon as possible. But there were no real leaders. The experts were all busy with the revision of the liturgical books. The pastoral renewal in the local churches lacked leaders whose theological, historical and pastoral knowledge could have prevented the mistakes and exaggerations that scandalized many people. I witnessed this revolution. Under the pretext of officially approved "experimentation" many abuses were committed, which disturbed some people and forced the authorities to react. So it is understandable that the Vatican took measures in the seventies to curtail the abuses. It seemed that because some people's experiments went too far, others thought that gradually everything ought to return to a centralized policy of the past, although the Council had quite clearly called our attention to the fact that the liturgy should be adapted to the local culture and usage of people and ethnic groups. But without competent leadership, the exaggerated zeal often led, on one hand, to mistakes and abuses, and resulted, on the other, in a certain ultra-conservative reaction.

Change is never easy. The changes desired and requested by Vatican II were not readily implemented. Even the official ecclesial authorities made mistakes. Some people expected too much from the revised liturgical books. Some people misunderstood the essence of the liturgy. Some believed that the liturgy would solve all our problems, even though the Council had clearly stated that the liturgy does not exhaust the whole Christian life, but is rather its source and summit. It does not even exhaust the spiritual life; it is but an essential part of it. We were such idealists after the Council that we wanted to produce a perfect liturgy. We did not realize that there is no such thing as perfect liturgy here on earth. Only in heaven will we have it. Here on earth we grow and ripen slowly on the road of historical development, towards the true and perfect liturgy, which will then be our joy in heaven.

Many were reluctant to implement the liturgical directives. We know how difficult it is to move, change or abandon age-old habits. It is not easy to conquer our love of comfort and, instead of a prescribed, uniform liturgy, to choose from among the many possibilities that which is most fitting under the circumstances. Many were unable to shed old (and often wrong) customs. In the past we had read the Latin liturgical texts in a barely audible voice, because "the people didn't understand them anyway"; when the language of the liturgy changed to the vernacular, we continued to read the liturgy in the same incomprehensible fashion. It was also a great mistake that we did not duly prepare people with some kind of catechesis to explain various changes: why we can now receive holy communion under both forms, why we can take the host in our hand instead of on our tongue, why we exchange a sign of peace, or why we once again include the prayer of the faithful, etc. Lacking such explanations, some people were reluctant to accept these small changes, which seemed like novelties to those who had little historical background, while others went to extremes. This uneasiness and confusion appeared not only in connection with the liturgy, but also in other fields of church life.

Authors like James Hitchcock suggest certain continuing difficulties with the liturgy: a loss of a sense of mystery, insensitivity to symbols, and the lack of a liturgical community. To heal these problems, so we might better implement the liturgical renewal, let's examine each area briefly.

Christianity is essentially mystery. Vatican II's *Dogmatic Constitution on the Church (Lumen Gentium)* emphasizes that the Church is mystery, and the liturgy is even more so. This supernatural mystery is closely connected with the mystery of the Incarnation. Only if we are willing to enter into such mystery can we approach it. Current trends lead us in the opposite direction, towards secularism, desacralisation, demythologization. Here is the conflict. Do we still need mystery today? Does it mean anything to modern people?

Romano Guardini, one of the leaders of the Liturgical Movement, asked towards the end of the sixties: Are people today still able to deal with liturgy, to be a liturgical people? Such questions are related to the problem of whether the concepts of the Holy, the Sacred, the Mystery have significance for modern humanity. In a secularized world when even the Church proposes adapting to local cultures, the dilemma emerges: How secular can we become? How important is it to preserve the sense of the Sacred, of the Mystery in the Church, especially within the liturgy? It is easy for adaptation to slip into assimilation, which often results when people become too caught up in the notion of relevance. Is it relevant? Is it pragmatic, practical, understandable for modern people? If these become the only criteria, then we simply discard that which is not relevant (and in the liturgy many things may neither be relevant nor correspond to the requirements of the present age).

In the early years after the Council, and still occasionally today, we hear that we should forget about liturgy; we shouldn't bother about building churches or performing rituals because these are superfluous. We should be addressing the real problems, social problems. This emphasis on social issues has sometimes pushed the concern for liturgy into the background. Yet, experience has shown that strong and vibrant liturgical life goes hand in hand with social responsibility, which has consequences in everyday life. In the United States, the Liturgical Weeks, held from 1930 on, were one of the most influential factors in the Liturgical Movement. Hundreds of priests, religious and laypeople participated every year, until 1969, when the Liturgical Week took place in Milwaukee. There the organizers decided that to study liturgy, participants should go to the slums to try to discover the residents' social needs and problems. While this is a very important task, it is not liturgy. When we try to make liturgy bear all the worries, concerns, social and political problems of the Church or the world, we lose liturgy's unique identity. This experiment brought an end to the Liturgical Weeks; people were no longer interested.

Liturgy is situated at the heart of the church's mission, from which it takes its special character. This mission includes the proclamation of the word of God *(kerygma)*, the celebration of the paschal mystery *(leitourgia)* and service to the community and the world *(diakonia)*. A fourth aspect of the Church's mission is to build up the community of the Church *(koinonia)*. Thus, within the Church's mission, liturgy is only one of four fundamental tasks. But even though all four are closely connected, they should not be confused with each other. The Church needs the liturgy to survive. Diakonia can never substitute for nor make the liturgy superfluous.

Unfortunately we have lost our sensitivity to liturgical symbols. In a highly pragmatic, rationalist world, it can be difficult for liturgical symbols, which serve no practical goal, to find their place. These symbols have their own meaning in themselves. It is interesting to note that some people are inclined to reject material things. This inclination might be called a form of neo-Montanism because people want to establish an immediate relationship with the spiritual, and so reject or fail to appreciate the incarnation, the embodiment of spirit in matter. Other people suggest that our age is seeing a renewal of the eighteenth-century Enlightenment, when people also wanted to introduce certain liturgical reforms, but which would have ultimately made the liturgy merely a didactic and rationalistic exercise. Every symbol, every mystery has been eliminated from the liturgy. Yet the world of symbols is a necessary component in the healthy development of a human being.

In the past liturgical communities were parish communities, which truly needed to be reformed. Many new ideas were designed to build up liturgical community, but failed. Perhaps this burden can be laid at the feet of a loss of connectedness with the past. If the past is considered burdensome and is therefore to be discarded, a community can develop neither a present nor a future. A common history is one of the strongest community-forming powers.

The disintegration of liturgical communities was also quickened by an emphasis on spontaneity, which plays a much greater role in today's world than in the past. People are looking for spontaneous expressions of their idiosyncratic spiritual experiences in liturgy. No doubt, such spontaneity may have its place and even an important role within liturgy, but if everyone wants to impose their own spiritual experience on the liturgy, then we can speak neither of community, nor of community-building liturgy. Subjective elements, experiences, feelings were so overemphasized that the liturgical community which was bound together by common ritual—connected not only with past Christian generations, but also with our brothers and sisters throughout the world today—was almost completely destroyed.

The sense of community was also lessened by the changing nature of people's relationship to authority in recent years, as they became less and less willing to follow a single set of rules. This is seen both on the right and left of the religious spectrum. It is interesting to observe in this context Luther's care that the implementation of his liturgical reform not lead to disruption. He said that our faith is looking to express itself spontaneously, to express externally whatever it feels internally. Yet, we cannot settle for that, because love, the binding element of the Christian community, demands that our worship be structured and have certain formulas.

Still another problem is ecclesiological, that is, a problem of who we are as church. During the years since Vatican II, many a small community or basic community has emerged in almost every part of the world. With wonderful ideas and great enthusiasm, they tried to establish genuine Christian communities. Unfortunately, in some places these basic communities soon went underground and separated from the body of the Church. Those communities, however, that had a healthy ecclesial spirituality have continued to flourish until today. How, therefore, can we integrate the so-called small communities, which cannot be neglected or overlooked in today's Church, into the larger parish-community so that they become living cells of the whole parish or diocese?

The purpose of this short historical introduction was to describe the present situation of the liturgy, to see its problems, and to lead us to think about the true renewal of the liturgy. The real liturgical renewal has not yet begun; the liturgical reform was not sufficient. The liturgical revolution called our attention to certain dangers and certain gaps. Now we should begin the true renewal by filling the forms with spirit, by helping each other, priests and people, to develop a liturgical spirituality. Only with this spirituality firmly anchored as the centre of our lives can the liturgical rites express the central mystery of the Christian life, the mystery of Christ. In this next phase of the liturgical renewal we will need to study the liturgy to understand, grasp, and sense what true liturgy is. It is important to establish the fundamental principles of liturgy, according to which we may be able to distinguish the essential components from the changing, variable elements. This will enable us to change without compromising the essentials.

The following chapters will deal with these fundamental theological principles of the liturgy. We will reflect on how we can recognize anew the mystery of faith; how we can better appreciate liturgical symbols; how we can restore the liturgical community. How can we make the liturgy the privileged place of humanity's encounter with God, where salvation history happens, where Jesus Christ continues his redeeming work in a special way? This is important not only for believers, but also for all those with whom we are in solidarity, that is, the whole world, yes, even the whole universe.

Part I

THEOLOGICAL PRINCIPLES OF THE LITURGY

Chapter 2

LITURGY: AN ENCOUNTER WITH THE SACRED

If we are to fill the revised forms with content, life and spirit, we must know what we are doing when we celebrate the liturgy. Thus we now turn to the theological principles of the liturgy. Reflecting on what liturgy is will enable us to deepen our understanding of its reality in our own lives, and communicate it to others. My aim in the following chapter is to describe, if not define, what liturgy is.

Liturgy is an encounter with the Sacred Reality. This is the essence of every act of worship, in both primitive religions, and the observation of liturgical experience. From this perspective, Christian liturgy is the same as worship in other religions, that is, an encounter with Sacred Reality.

To analyze what this description means, we must first clarify what we mean by *encounter*. Theologians began to use this concept in the 1960s to explain that in the celebration of liturgy we have an encounter here, an encounter between God and a human person. Many people still think the old way and expect that the sacraments distribute grace to them. The priest does not "dispense" sacraments as if grace could be distributed as a tangible, measurable thing. Sacraments involve a personal relationship, communication, participation in the life of the other, which eventually may even lead to the union of the persons involved. When we speak about *encounter* in the liturgy, in reality we mean an encounter in which human beings participate in God's life and in love. This is what we call "grace."

Such an encounter with God always gives rise to a religious experience. According to philosophers or psychologists of religion, such an experience, if genuine, entails an encounter with an objective reality. It is not merely some kind of subjective feeling, but an encounter that engages the whole human person, body and soul, intellect and will, heart and emotions. It deals with the deepest human existential problems, questions that interest everyone, believers and nonbelievers equally. Such problems are: Where do we come from? Where do we go to? How do we relate to evil in the world? How can we overcome this evil? Is there any great being above the world in whose hands our lives are held? ... and so forth. This experience usually happens in a form of dialogue, in an exchange that moves in two directions: upward and downward. The upward movement, in which human beings open themselves towards the other world, the transcendent Reality, is our part. It is usually called adoration or worship. We open up towards the Infinite and remain open to receive more and greater things than ourselves. This is the anthropological aspect of worship.

This upward movement, however, is only one half of the encounter. The downward movement is even more important. It comes from above, from the Sacred Reality, from God. This movement is usually described as our sanctification or participation in God's sacred being. God communicates to us grace, love and life, because God is Love who is constantly pouring out and revealing the divine self. Revelation, then, is not just the communication of certain teachings or laws, but the communication of God's very life through words and deeds. This, too, we name "grace."

The uniqueness of the liturgy consists precisely in the fact that it is comprised not only of our human activities, but also of God's mysterious actions. Liturgy is not merely "human work" (*opus hominis*); it is primarily "God's work" (*opus Dei*). The mystery we call liturgy consists in the mysterious blending of divine and human activity in ways that are scarcely distinguishable from one another. It is important to emphasize this mysterious, mystery-character of the liturgy. Considered merely from the viewpoint of the human sciences (anthropology, psychology, sociology, etc.), liturgy would at most seem to be what human beings do, but we could not say much about how God enters our lives when our acts of worship are joined and combined with God's acts. Liturgy is therefore mystery, the continuation of the mystery of the Incarnation, and the interconnectedness of the divine and human that the human intellect cannot grasp.

In the first half of the twentieth century, Rudolf Otto emphasized, in contrast to many philosophers and historians of religion, that there is no religious experience without an objective Sacred. Thus he successfully opposed the subjectivist interpretation of religion which saw human religiosity only in terms of subjective feelings. Otto then analyzed this Sacred as it is found among primitive peoples and in all religions. While Christians name the Sacred "God," Otto names this reality "*Numen*," because this Sacred is full of light and glory. The concept of "holy" may express best what primitive people and we ourselves mean by God: the One who is full of light and glory; whose power is mighty because he holds the whole world in his hands; who above all is irresistibly attractive.

Otto describes four characteristics of the Sacred. First, the Sacred is physically unapproachable, i.e., far from our world of experience: in the language of philosophy, "transcendent." This unapproachability awakens in human beings an attitude of utter reverence and even fear, the fear of God (*timor Dei*), which Scripture describes as one of the gifts of the Holy Spirit. Since today we prefer to emphasize that God awakens in us love, not fear, we hear little of the fear of God as a component of our religious experience. Yet, it is important to realize that because the Sacred is so high and so unapproachable, we can only approach the Sacred out of a healthy fear of God.

Second, the Sacred is overwhelming in power and majesty. The Sacred is so overwhelming that before God's majesty, humans feel their nothingness, their creaturehood, their continuous and radical dependence on God. The saints expressed it this way: "You are everything, I am nothing!"

Third, the Sacred is full of dynamism and energy. This is no monolith, no pillar of stone, but the living God, full of vitality, brimming over with the energy of life. This is the God who, according to the Old Testament, is "devouring fire." To this God, humans respond with a certain excitement and enthusiasm. We do not simply gaze upon the Sacred; rather, God's dynamic power rouses us to action.

Fourth, the Sacred is mysterious. The Sacred is true mystery, for it can neither be understood nor comprehended: it is unpronounceable (*ineffabilis*). Our intellect cannot understand this Being who is always shrouded in mystery. To this mystery, humans respond with wonder. We stand in awe before the One who defies our intellectual understanding.

Taken alone, these four characteristics of the Sacred may seem oppressive; they might lead us to an image of God that fills us only with fear and trembling (*tremendum*). But there is a fifth characteristic of the Sacred: the Sacred is infinitely fascinating (*fascinosum*). In its power, majesty and inapproachability, the Sacred is wonderfully attractive. Like Moses before the burning bush, we cannot escape its magic attraction. This fascination awakens in our hearts the desire and love that gradually draw us into unity with the Sacred, which we encounter in our religious experience.

The Sacred is a spiritual being whom our senses cannot perceive, but with whom we are connected. Such a connection is possible only if the Sacred reveals itself to us by its own will and appears in different forms in the human sphere. The science of religion calls the various apparitions of the Sacred theophanies, or hierophanies. The Sacred can choose to reveal this divine presence in many different forms; the science of religion recognizes hundreds of such theophanies: nature, the sky, the sun, the moon, the stars; different plants or animals, the person of a king, ancestors, etc. The Sacred appears in time and space; we have sacred times, such as the morning and evening hours, or holy days or holy seasons. The Sacred appears at holy places: on a mountaintop, at a fountain, a lakeside, a rock or a tree. The Sacred may communicate through holy things. Finally, the most important form of such revelation is history itself. We can thus speak of a "salvation history" in the Old and New Testament, because through the events of human history the Sacred is revealed in words, deeds and events.

Human beings respond to these theophanies in external forms that the senses can grasp. When the phenomenology of religion studies these forms of expression of religious experience, it examines how human beings manifest their religious experiences: words, such as prayers, creeds, dogmatic formulations and holy scriptures; and actions, gestures, postures and rituals (which combine words and actions). These ultimately lead to the development of complex rites of sacrifice, purification, reconciliation and sacred meals. These manifestations of religious experience are normally communal, and normally happen within the framework of a community that is held together by its common religious experience and common ritual.

These primitive elements are also found in Christian liturgy. From the perspective of the phenomenology of religion, we can say that liturgy is the external and communal manifestation of our previous religious experiences. If this is true, then liturgy will become good liturgy only if the rituals and prayers contain and truly manifest the participants' individual and communal religious experience. This means that we will not have good liturgy if, without preparation or previous religious experience, we just expect something will happen. We need to bring to liturgy our whole life, our religiosity, our devotions, our surrender from the first moment of our lives until now. Then, during communal liturgical events, visible, audible, tangible liturgical symbols can manifest both human responses and the grace and love of God in one mysterious event of God's grace.

Contemporary believers find the relationship of the sacred and profane particularly problematic as they deal with a secularized worldview. The late French Dominican theologian (and later cardinal) Yves Congar explains the issue very well, tracing the evolution of secularization in the scriptures themselves. First, Congar explains, the pantheism of the ancient pagan world considered the whole world divine, because God was supposed to be everywhere: in shrubs, animals, people. As the emanation of the divinity, the world was sacred. In the midst of this pagan world then appear the creation accounts of the Old Testament, which clearly state that the world is not God, not divine, not sacred, but "worldly," secular. The creation story thus secularized the world. The world is not opposed to the divine, the sacred; rather it is neutral territory. The only opposition or enemy of the Sacred is sin, which makes the world "profane." Creation, the world, the cosmos are neutral. This is the teaching of the creation story in the Old Testament.

Throughout history, God chose Israel; this election begins a new process of sacralisation. Set apart for holiness and consecrated as

God's people, God's holy people were surrounded by all kinds of boundaries and regulations. This holiness appeared in different degrees. Think of the different courts in the Temple of Jerusalem, each indicating different degrees of holiness and the many minute regulations that tried to defend the sacred from the profane. Thus the Old Testament maintained a sharp division between the holy and the profane. But when Jesus Christ came into this world, he broke down the wall separating sacred and profane. Israel was concerned with holy days, holy places, holy persons, but Christ did not restrict the sphere of the sacred to one people, certain persons, certain places, such as the Temple of Jerusalem, or certain days such as the Sabbath. Because the "holy" is universal, it can include everything. A note of caution is in order: Christ did not suggest that everything is sacred to the same degree, but that everything can and should become divine. This ultimate goal of Christ's mission extends not only to humanity, but also to the whole cosmos.

Not everything is holy to the same degree in the New Testament, but, following Yves Congar's reflections, we can distinguish four degrees of holiness.

1. The body of Christ

The only Sacred Reality is God who is a spiritual being, not an earthly reality. Yet, here on earth we recognize an absolute Sacred Reality, which is tangible and concrete. It appears in historical form: the body of Christ. According to the dogma of the Incarnation, the body which Christ took from the Blessed Virgin Mary is the body of the Second Divine Person; and so through the hypostatic union it is the absolute Sacred Reality, the only absolute Sacred Reality here on earth. According to Scripture, however, the body of Christ should be considered in its threefold manifestation. First, it refers to the physical body which Christ received from the Blessed Virgin Mary. Thus he lived here among us for thirty-three years, and we could touch him and be touched by him; now, this body, risen and glorified, sits at the right hand of the Father. This is the first meaning of the body of Christ. Second, it refers to Christ's eucharistic body. According to the dogma of the Eucharist, Christ is present truly, really, substantially, and in a tangible way present under the species of bread and wine. Here too we must recognize the Absolute Sacred Reality. Third, the mystical, ecclesial body of Christ is also a concrete, sensible reality, although it is not always so easy to localize it. These three manifestations of the body of Christ are inseparable from each other. Wherever the body of Christ is present, there is his real body, which walked among us on earth and now sits at the right hand of the Father. This same body is also given to us in the Eucharist. The Church as Christ's body continues Christ's life in a communal mode. Thus, the body of Christ is the only Absolute Sacred Reality among us: it is the truly "Holy." The other degrees of the Holy are all related to this Absolute Sacred Reality.

2. Sacramental encounters with Christ

Sacraments, that is, sacramental encounters with Christ and their permanent consequences, the sacramental status, constitute the second degree of the holy. It is neither the baptismal water nor the oil of the sick in themselves that are the sacraments, but the sacramental encounters with Christ manifested in concrete form through the sacramental action: sins are forgiven, the sick are anointed, bride and groom are joined in marriage. In the sacramental action we meet Christ; consequently, those who participate in this sacramental encounter are sanctified, become "holy." This is why St. Paul can tell the Corinthians that they are saints: because they are baptized. Similarly couples who are married in Christ become holy.

3. Liturgical symbols and signs

Liturgical symbols and signs comprise the third degree of the "Holy." These liturgical symbols, which assist the sacramental encounter with Christ, are usually pedagogical tools that create the milieu of the sacramental encounter. We call them pedagogical instruments because they have no absolute value; they are not necessarily useful in every age. These signs ought to be evaluated periodically and, if necessary, changed. The world of liturgical symbols belongs so completely to the nature of human beings that it would be difficult, if not impossible, to imagine a sacramental encounter without them. Our sacramental rituals are full of these symbols. Take for example, baptism. The only essential element is that water be poured on the candidate's head accompanied by the words "I baptize you in the name of the Father ..." Yet how many other symbols surround this central action: the scriptural texts, the candle, the white garment and the anointing with oil. All these liturgical symbols form the milieu in which the religious experience of the candidates is expressed and their response to God's self-communication in these symbols is manifested.

4. The created world

The whole created world is the fourth degree of the "Holy." Christ abolished the separation between sacred and profane, because he made it possible for the whole world to become holy, and even intimated that it *should* become holy, that it should enter into God's life. This is the task of the human person: to make the world holy, to sanctify it, to lead all humanity and the whole cosmos into the life of God. This does not mean that we sprinkle everything with holy water, but that our sacred symbols (sacramentals) promote the sanctification of the world when we use created things prudently and rightly. Thus, the whole created world can gradually become a liturgical symbol, that is, a milieu in which encountering Christ becomes, not only possible, but also easy. Then, in the sacramental encounter we will be united with the eucharistic and ecclesial body of Christ, in which we are already with God, the Absolute Sacred Reality.

Grasping this sense of the Holy is still not enough. We cannot really celebrate the liturgy if our image of God is faulty, or if we do not believe in God, because our understanding of God goes beyond a universally accepted "Sacred Reality." Liturgy is useless for those who do not believe in Christ, and in his Incarnation, with all of its consequences. Nor can we truly celebrate the liturgy if we do not believe in the Church, since liturgy is the action of the Church. To truly celebrate liturgy well, we must first ask ourselves whether our images of God and Christ are authentic. We will also have to examine how we believe in the Incarnation, and what our relationship to and love for the church is. We turn to these questions in our next chapter.

Chapter 3

LITURGY: ACKNOWLEDGEMENT OF THE CREATOR AND COVENANT GOD

In every liturgical action there is an encounter between God and human beings. Such an encounter with the Sacred Reality calls for that absolute reverence and adoration that we already find among primitive peoples. In a liturgical context, this suggests that our attitude must manifest our recognition of the "Holy." We experience this unique Absolute Sacred Reality not only in the Eucharist, but also in the other sacred actions.

Every liturgical action expresses our inner, cumulative religious experience. Our liturgy will be truly eventful and enjoyable for individuals and for the community if we bring to the liturgy and express there our previous religious experience. Without such religious experience, it will be difficult to expect good and effective liturgy. Only rarely does someone who has no preparation receive from the liturgy a decisive experience of God, as did Paul Claudel. Such an event is an exception. Good liturgy is produced by the faithful whose religious experiences and expressions of that experience are a major component of true liturgy.

This is especially true of the experience of God. Since liturgy is the acknowledgement of the Creator and Covenant God, our image of God is very important. Yet it is never easy to construct. Because liturgy is the Christian community's worship, the image of God we receive from tradition about God is significant. According to this common image, each individual forms the image of God for themselves. Therefore we must go back to the Old Testament to rediscover Israel's experience and image of God.

Israel's fundamental religious experience was the Exodus event, its liberation from Egypt. In that event the people of Israel began to be aware that their God walks with them, cares for them, and, for some strange reason, loves them. Yahweh[1] is their national God who leads them out of slavery, guides them through the desert, through the Red Sea, and enters into covenant with them at Mount Sinai, a life-covenant that the sacred writers described as a marriage. At the covenant of Sinai, Israel realized that the Lord is their God who saved them, to whom they belong, to whom their life is joined, whose people they are. In this happy knowledge Israel lived for centuries in the Promised Land until national catastrophe befell them.

First, the Assyrians and, later, the Babylonians, flooded into Israel and almost annihilated the Israelites by deporting them into hard slavery. A spiritual crisis erupted in Israel as the people began to reason: We have a God, but it seems that our national God either doesn't love us anymore, or can't defend us against the Assyrians and Babylonians. In the midst of this crisis of faith the prophets emerged: first Isaiah, then Jeremiah, and the others. Through the prophets the Lord reveals to the people that the Lord is the God, not only of Israel, but also of the Assyrians and Babylonians, the Phoenicians, and every nation—including Israel's enemies. All the nations of the world belong to the Lord because he is Lord of all peoples. The prophetic utterances go even further in correcting Israel's image of God: Israel slowly begins to realize, especially during the Babylonian exile, that their God, the Lord whom they know from personal and historical experience, is not only their God and the God of all peoples, but also the God of the whole universe. It was the Lord who created the sun and the moon and the stars, including Baal and Marduk. Everything that exists in heaven and on earth comes from the Lord's creative hand. He is absolute Lord above everything. Thus, Israel came to understand that the Lord is the Creator God. Redemption, not creation, is Israel's first experience of God.

---

[1] While I am mindful that Jewish people do not speak the Holy Name, I prefer to use it because this is the personal name of Israel's God and indicates God's special, familiar relationship with Israel (and us). *Adonai* or Lord refers more to God as Creator. My point is that God is both all-powerful creator (Lord) and loving Father (YHWH) at the same time.

First Israel experiences that the LORD loves, redeems, and liberates them. Only then does it acknowledge that this national God is also the God of the whole universe, the Creator God.

Israel's basic experience of God is expressed in the formula we find in Deuteronomy: "Hear, O Israel, the LORD is our God, the LORD alone." This brief formula is the foundation of Israel's belief and life. It is familiar in Christian circles because, in response to the scribe's question about the most important commandment, Jesus quoted this text together with the following verses: "You shall love the Lord your God with all your heart and with all your soul and with all your mind. Keep these words that I am commanding today in your heart. Recite them to your children and talk about them when you are at home and when you are away, when you lie down and when you rise. Bind them as a sign on your hand, fix them as an emblem on your forehead, and write them on the doorposts of your house and on your gates" (Deut. 6:4-9). This is the famous *shema*, Israel's basic creed. According to Jesus, this is the first and main commandment. Jews and Christians share faith in the same God.

We should mark this text well: the LORD, our God, is the only God. According to the Hebrew text, "the LORD" is God's personal name. When we say that the LORD is "*our* God," then we profess our personal relationship with the LORD as God of our nation. But at the same time we also profess the LORD as the God of the whole universe, because the LORD is the only God: there is no other. Baal, Marduk and the others are not gods. Everything comes from the one God, Creator and Almighty who is Lord above everything. This monotheistic belief in the one God is so deeply imbedded in the spirituality of Israel that, in the Jewish liturgy, no ritual or prayer is imaginable without the *shema*. Up to our days, the *shema* is the central part of every Jewish liturgical action; it permeates Jewish private prayer, too. Not only do observant Jews know this text by heart, but they also write this text on a parchment that they tie on their forehead and arm during prayer, and place on the door-posts of their homes, so that by touching it as they go out or come in, they may remember their profession of faith. True Israelites live and die with this; they repeat it many times during the day, and die with this text on their lips: *Shema Israel, YHWH Elohenu, YHWH Ehad* (Listen, Israel: the LORD, our God, is the Only God!).

Christians received this basic concept of God from Israel through Jesus Christ and our own tradition. The statement, "our God is the only God" means that he is Lord above all. The very concept of "God" means that God can do whatever God wants, without being subject to anyone. No one can call God to account for what or why God is doing something. This can shock us unless we realize that one of our biggest problems in believing in God is that we always imagine God in human terms. Two extremes tend to emerge: an image of God as a tyrant who sits somewhere on high, ready to punish people whenever they offend these laws, or God as a jolly old man whose only concern is to bring candies and lollipops to children and occasionally pat us on the head. These two extremes were already known to Israel. But the right image of God harmoniously combines these images.

To this fundamental profession of faith comes a liturgical response that Israel repeats from the beginning, and this constitutes the foundation of their liturgy: Blessing God! In Hebrew, this is called *berakah*. When the people of Israel begin to pray, the prayer always begins with this blessing of God: "Blessed are you, the LORD, our God, king of the universe!" Thus, we find the liturgical expression of their profession of faith at the beginning and end of every prayer. In fact, this is the traditional prayer formula of the Old and New Testament. Every prayer should begin by blessing God, acknowledging that he is the king of the whole universe, professing that he is the only God, the only Lord.

The almighty and omnipotent God is also the loving Father who knows best how to care for his children. The mystery of the One God consists in the fact that he can be both Lord above all and loving Father: mysterious, incomprehensible—God. Israel recognizes this when it addresses the one God: *Abinu, Malkenu!*, that is: "Our Father, and our King!" The unity of these two images in one God is at the heart of the mystery of God. This is the first article of our creed, too: "I believe in one God, the Father almighty, Creator of heaven and earth!" Without this fundamental image of God the remaining articles of our faith make little sense, because the whole redeeming work of Christ, his death on the cross and his resurrection, are all based on it.

Without this fundamental statement of belief and this harmonious image of God as part of their lived reality, people will constantly experience some difficulty believing or even a crisis of faith. How can we explain, for instance, one of the most difficult existential problems of our life: Why must the innocent suffer? When a little child is sick and nobody can help him, when a young mother of several children is dying of cancer, when tens of thousands of people perish in a few minutes during an earthquake, what kind of answers can we give? Can we say that God is a cruel tyrant, or a nice old grandpa who watches the children? There is no other answer than our conviction that our God is both a loving Father and the omnipotent Lord who can do whatever he wants. We cannot even question why. To these difficult problems the only response is that God is Lord who can do everything, not just as an omnipotent God, but also as a loving Father in whom we ought to trust blindly, and in whose hands we ought to place our lives, because our God takes care of us and always wants the best for us. His mysterious ways are inscrutable: "My ways are not your ways." If we understood everything God does or allows, God would not be God.

This question of the right image of God is the main concern of one of the most poetic books of the Old Testament, the Book of Job. Job, whom we know to be a just man, experiences all kinds of trials. He loses his family and his assets; he is beset with all kinds of sicknesses, and is finally sequestered on a dung heap where his friends try to console him: "Look, Job, all these things happened to you because you hold yourself a just man. If you would just confess that you are a sinner, and acknowledge that God punishes you for your sins, then everything would be all right. All these misfortunes have befallen because you have sinned." But Job rejects both this accusation and their reasoning. He insists that he is righteous, and asks why God still punishes him. Job even curses the day of his birth and wants to take God to court for being unjust with him. In chapters 38 to 42, the Lord answers Job out of the whirlwind: Who are you, Job, that you dare to question me? Rather than answer Job's question, God asks Job: "Who are you, that you dare to call me to court? Where were you when I created the world?" That is, God reminds Job that God alone is the Creator of all. To this, Job can only say: "Look, I am nothing. What can I say to you? I put my finger to my lips. I have spoken once and now will not answer again ... Now I see you with my own eyes and realize that you can do all things. There is nothing impossible for you. I have spoken of great things which I have not understood, things too wonderful for me to know. I knew of you only by report, but now I see you with my own eyes. Therefore I melt away, I repent in dust and ashes."

In acknowledging this God, Job suddenly realizes what the right image of God is. God can do whatever God wants; I cannot even ask why and how. This image would be quite frightening if it were not complemented by other images that show different aspects of this same God who speaks to us through the prophets and through his holy Son: "You are precious to me; I love you with an everlasting love; I call you by name, you are mine; I have chosen you to myself, I enter into a marriage covenant with you; I draw you to myself." The combination of these images brings us to the right concept of God.

Israel's recognition that the LORD, our God, is the Only God, the Creator God, resulted in the liturgy of Israel, Jewish worship. As creatures we depend utterly on God. The dogma of creation belongs to the first article of our Creed, upon which the rest of our belief is built. Creation, however, does not mean merely that some thousands of years ago God started the movement of the world and then left it to itself. Creation means that God continuously creates us: that is, we are always radically dependent on him. Our worship is recognition of this relationship between Creator and creature and acknowledgement of who our God is.

The first and basic task of every creature is to recognize this relationship of dependence, and to profess what the principal Old Testament commandment says: the LORD, our God, is the Only God, and there is no other. It is most important to also admit that we are neither God, nor God's rivals. I am not God's rival. Here our concept of God cuts into the flesh, for this is our constant temptation; even the psalmist recognizes that the Lord created us *almost* as gods. According to the biblical account, the primordial sin of Adam and Eve was wanting to be like God, wanting to know as much as God knows. This remains at the root of every sin: human beings want to be god, and don't accept that the LORD is the only God. Our perennial temptation is to

Liturgy: Acknowledgement of the Creator and Covenant God

consider ourselves the centre of the world. This is the primordial sin deeply rooted in all of us.

Whenever we acknowledge and revere God, when we confess using the words of the creed that the Creator is the only God, we also say that we are not God. And with this we make the basic sacrifice of our lives: we bless God! Every human being is obliged to offer this fundamental sacrifice. Without it there is no real worship of God, no real prayer, no real liturgy. "To bless God" (i.e., to say *berakah*) means to acknowledge the LORD as the only God and myself as a creature. Together with the angels we bless, praise, glorify, acknowledge, and sanctify God: Holy, Holy, Holy are you, Lord of the universe, almighty God! This recognition is the origin of the medieval Latin expression, the "sacrifice of praise" (*sacrificium laudis*) which identifies self-surrender as the fundamental creaturely sacrifice.

This attitude opens our hearts, making it possible for God's self-communication and love to pour into and sanctify us. This openness towards God can happen in different degrees; throughout our lives we should try to grow in our openness to God so that at the moment of death we can perform the most important act of worship of our whole life: our complete surrender to God.

This attitude is the foundation of every liturgical action. Without it there can be no genuine liturgy, be it baptism, reconciliation, Eucharist, liturgy of the hours, or anything else. Such worship is not a matter of doing what we like when we feel like it; rather, it is a task, a duty, (*officium laudis*) that belongs to the essence of our creaturehood.

Such worship, because it acknowledges our radical creaturely dependence on God, also reveals other aspects of our identity as human creatures. First, we are persons, unique beings. Among the billions of people on earth no two persons are the same, not even twins. Every human person is unique and enjoys a unique relationship with God. Therefore we cannot, and must not, be jammed together into some kind of anonymous crowd where we lose our individual personality. This uniqueness obliges us to maintain our individual, private contact with God. This is why every liturgy presupposes our individual religious experience along with our obligation to communal liturgy. As persons we also have intellects that should be brought to bear on our prayer life, religious life and meditation. Persons possess free will that we ought to use to grow in love towards God and other human beings. Likewise, our emotions should also be engaged in the liturgy. Liturgy therefore engages the intellectual, volitional, and emotional aspects of the human person because only in this way will the whole person be able to respond to God.

Our creaturehood also shows that we are social beings who cannot survive without other persons. Blood relationships and psychological bonds join us to the whole human race. In the liturgy this solidarity means that we respond to God communally. Our reflections on the Church as the Mystical Body of Christ in Chapter 6 will make this more meaningful. As creatures we must turn to God not only individually, but with others, with the whole human race. Whether we like it or not, we always influence the lives of others. Social responsibility is, therefore, an essential part of who we are when we celebrate liturgy.

God wanted, planned and created us to consist of body and spirit. Why did God make us such wondrous beings in whom the material and spiritual worlds form an essential, substantial, inseparable unity? The anthropological dogma of the Church clearly teaches that we are dealing here with substantial unity. This rather dry statement has far-reaching consequences. It means that, throughout our whole existence, we are essentially connected with matter. (This may sound novel because the influence of Plato has led us to think that we become more perfect if we are freed from matter.) From a liturgical viewpoint, the consequence of this dogma is that the truly perfect human act of worship is not one that is merely spiritual and intellectual, but one that comes from the soul and manifests itself in matter, that is, it expresses religious experience in a visible, audible, tangible, and sensible way. Soul and spirit are incarnate, embodied.

Being creatures means that God created us as historical beings. We do not come into the world as mature persons, but (as St. Irenaeus says) we were born as babies (*nepios*). We begin our earthly life as embryos; only slowly do we develop, passing through childhood and youth to a ripe adulthood and, finally, old age. Growing and developing in history is God's will for us. We are always incomplete, looking ahead, open to the future. Therefore here on earth we will never have a perfect liturgy, because we are always on the road. It is important to keep this before our eyes, especially as we meditate on the meaning of old age. To most people old age seems a curse and burden, something outside of God's plan. If we truly believe that God's wisdom is expressed in his creation, then we must admit that God's plan also includes the process of aging. As our bodies weaken, and our circle of friends and relatives narrows, we focus on the crowning event of our life, the final act that is the only true answer to God's self-communicating revelation: the moment of death when we place ourselves completely in God's hands.

Our liturgy acknowledges this God of creation and covenant. We acknowledge God's holiness, and bless, praise, and celebrate God in the liturgy. We praise God in the various doxologies: "Glory to the Father, and to the Son, and to the Holy Spirit ...", "Glory to God in the highest ..." etc. When we celebrate, we recognize joyfully that we are creatures, God's creatures, and joyfully profess that the LORD alone is our God. We proclaim God's praise when we sing the Alleluia: We praise God! Alleluia! Even as we joyfully acknowledge God for who he is, we remember our creaturehood and surrender ourselves to God in our sacrifice of praise.

This fundamental attitude of worship is ultimately manifested in the redeeming actions of the Lord Jesus, climaxing in his death on the cross. The first Adam failed to acknowledge God, so Christ, in his human nature, acknowledges God's majesty, holiness, uniqueness by surrendering his life into the Father's hands: "Father, into your hands I lay down my life!" It is on this cornerstone that all our liturgical action is built.

Chapter 4

LITURGY: THE EXERCISE OF THE PRIESTHOOD OF CHRIST

Our understanding of Christian liturgy must include the person and salvific work of Jesus Christ, because the liturgy is not only an encounter with the Sacred Reality, not only the acknowledgement of the Creator and Covenant God, but also—according to Vatican II (SC.7)—the exercise of the priesthood of Christ.

What do we understand by priesthood? The history of religion indicates that the concept of priesthood is strictly connected with the concepts of sacrifice and mediation. Priests are those persons who offer sacrifice and mediate. In this sense, we can say that every human being is a priest according to God's creative will. We could call this priesthood "natural" because God created human beings to offer sacrifice and be mediators.

As we noted in the previous chapter, the first duty of every human being is to acknowledge their creaturehood and surrender themselves into God's hands as a "sacrifice of praise" *(sacrificium laudis)*. Thus every human person is a priest because we all must offer this sacrifice. Only through this sacrifice can we establish a relationship with God.

The second task of the priesthood is to mediate. Created by God as social beings, we always influence other human beings and they influence us. Because of this inescapable solidarity our lives always mediate salvation or perdition. United with God through our sacrifice, we can then, explicitly or implicitly, mediate God's life and love to others.

As well as mediating to others, we mediate to the material world, the cosmos. Our bodies, spirit and matter that they are, place us in solidarity with the material world. Christian theology recalls that Christ came to redeem not only the human race, but also the whole universe. The whole cosmos is waiting with eager expectation to be freed from the shackles of slavery and to be introduced into the life of God's kingdom (cf. Rom.8). This, however, is possible only through human beings, those creatures who unite in themselves the spiritual and material worlds. This mediation with the cosmos is an important part of our human vocation.

Every contact with the material world happens through our senses, through which the cosmos becomes part of our personal life, so that we can carry it to God with whom our spiritual nature connects us. We can assimilate the material world through our senses and through various activities, such as eating. Through this process we mediate God's life to the cosmos, and return with the praise the cosmos offers God. Our liturgy speaks this cosmic praise of God. The Eastern liturgy in particular pays great attention to that fact that not only do human beings express God's praise, but all creation praises God through our voice.

Thus, an integral aspect of the human person is that he or she has been created priest both to offer sacrifice and, after the sacrifice is offered, to mediate between the human and material world. This is the ultimate existential meaning of our whole Christian life, since all Christians are called to exercise this natural priestly service. When human beings refuse to surrender themselves to God, or set themselves up as the centre of the universe, they sever their relationship with God, and cannot assume their roles as mediators. Such a posture frustrates both this fundamental human vocation and the ability of the world to reach the goal for which it has been created. Thus evil arises as the consequence of sin. God has assigned to all of us a portion of this material and human world, for which we as priests are responsible. Out of this "natural priesthood" flows the understanding of our baptismal priesthood. We speak therefore of this existential priesthood and existential sacrifice, and of our role as mediators which follows from our priesthood.

God's creative plan was frustrated by the primordial sin of the first human beings who refused to acknowledge, bless and praise God. Consequently the human race lost its connection with God, and its role as mediator became impossible. Human beings were unable to do that for which God had created them. The whole Old Testament illustrates how human beings tried, but were unable to restore this connection by their own power. In the fullness of time God came among us in the self-surrender of Jesus Christ in the Incarnation to bridge the abyss that our primordial sin had created.

Through the Incarnation, in the person of Jesus Christ, divine and human natures are united inseparably; Christ's very person bridges the divine and human worlds, reuniting them. This is why we call Christ *"Pontifex,"* bridge-builder or High Priest. Through the person of Christ the invisible divinity becomes a visible, tangible reality. Through the body of Christ, God is present among us: Emmanuel, God-with-us. This is why we say that Christ is the *Ursakrament,* the basic sacrament, the visible reality that includes and expresses the invisible reality.

In the liturgy, Christ the High Priest restores the exercise of our natural priestly service by offering his own sacrifice so that he might mediate between God and the human world, and God and the cosmos. As the basic sacrament, he belongs to both worlds, so he can both lead us to God the Father and mediate God's life to us.

Our tradition tells us that the exercise of Christ's priesthood happens primarily through the offering of his sacrifice. This sacrifice is nothing other than the paschal mystery, the mystery of Easter. With Vatican II we rediscovered this central tenet of the early Christian experience and belief, and today both Catholics and Protestants consider it the centre of liturgical life. Vatican II repeatedly mentions that in the liturgy the paschal mystery of Jesus Christ is made present, so that we might enter into this mystery and let it become a reality in our everyday life. (Cf. SC. 5–13).

There are four elements in the paschal mystery: the death of Christ, his resurrection, his ascension, and the outpouring of the Holy Spirit. Theologically these four elements constitute a unity. Only because of our limited capacity to perceive the mystery is this one mystical event celebrated chronologically as four events: Good Friday, Easter

Sunday, Ascension, and Pentecost. They mark the unfolding of the fifty days of the feast Easter, *Paschatis Sollemnia*. The connection between these 4 constitutive elements can be approached in the following way. On the cross, Christ, by his self-offering in death, perfectly acknowledges God's omnipotence, holiness, uniqueness, that is, he praises God *(berakah)*. This self-offering is the climax, not only of the whole passion story, but of Christ's whole life. We know well that the moving force behind everything the Lord did was "doing the Father's will." And when his hour had come in the Garden of Gethsemani, oppressed by the fear of death and anticipating the suffering connected with it, Jesus finishes his prayer: "Not my will, but yours be done" (Lk.22:42). Here we see the true sacrifice, the sacrifice of obedient love and surrender. The same thing is repeated on the cross, when Christ, abandoned by all, expressed his inner attitude in this way: "Father, into your hands I commend my spirit" (Lk.23:46).

With these words taken from Psalm 32, which are taught to Jewish children by their mothers as part of evening prayer, Jesus Christ expressed his total surrender, his basic sacrifice as a human being. With this surrender he offered the sacrifice of his life. Similarly, only in the moment of our own death will we be able to make this perfect sacrifice. Only in the moment of death can we throw ourselves completely into God's hands. And when we completely surrender, then divine life can stream into us and permeate our whole being: then we experience the new life of resurrection. When we completely abandon ourselves, then death becomes life, and we truly begin to live. True life comes to us through death alone. This is the paschal mystery.

The other two elements of the paschal mystery are the mystery of Ascension and Pentecost. The mystery of Ascension indicates that the life in which we participate after death is not merely the continuation of our life on earth, but truly a sharing in the divine life. We are all immersed into that Trinitarian life that flows among the three divine persons. But we can go still further. When we participate in this new divine life through death and resurrection, our life becomes both richer and superabundant. I can give it to others; I can radiate God's Spirit, the Holy Spirit, towards others.

It is important to note that these four elements of the paschal mystery constitute a unit. The unity can already be detected in John's gospel when the Lord Jesus on the cross breathes his last. According to the scripture scholars the expression *paredoken to pneuma* means not only that he gave up his spirit (that is, he died), but also that he gave us his Holy Spirit, the last element in our paschal transformation. Not only will we have life again, but we will become life-givers, Spirit-givers through the transforming power of the paschal mystery.

We will participate in the paschal mystery in full measure only in the moment of our death, but we can prepare for this moment during our earthly life. We often experience the paschal mystery partially, for ultimately it is the essence of our Christian existence, asceticism and life of virtue. Each time when we renounce a little bit of ourselves, that is, when we die to ourselves, to our ego and our selfishness, we already participate in the paschal mystery. On these occasions we begin to live a new life, a divinised life, and become more fully Spirit-givers. The paschal mystery, thus manifested in everyday ascetic and moral life, appears in a very special and dense way in every liturgical event, especially in the Eucharist. In every liturgy the mystery of Christ becomes present, and he invites us into his mystery. Thus every Mass and every liturgy will become fruitful for us inasmuch as we get involved in this paschal transformation. This is true for all the sacraments. In each case we experience the paschal mystery inasmuch as our present surrender *(devotio)* permits.

Christ's priestly ministry has further consequences. Christ did not just built a bridge through his incarnation and priestly sacrifice so that our communication with God might be restored, but invited us to be parts of his bridge, to actively and consciously participate in his priestly, sacrificial, mediatory ministry. He offers this invitation in the sacrament of baptism, when we are grafted onto the body of Christ to live his life and continue his work. This vocation of every Christian restores God's original plan. Thus human persons can once again become perfect and happy. Each Christian is called to exercise this common, baptismal priesthood in every liturgy. That is why the liturgical movement and Vatican II emphasized the conscious, active, fruitful participation of every Christian in the liturgical action: we celebrate God's greatness, uniqueness and goodness; we acknowledge God as our Lord and Creator; we surrender ourselves to him in Christ and with Christ to fulfil our role as mediators with the cosmos and the human world. Active participation in the liturgy refers primarily to this inner activity. External actions simply manifest this inner activity through different forms and services. The real activity, however, happens in the depths of our souls when we are united to Christ's paschal mystery.

One of the main tasks of the ministerial priesthood is to help develop the priesthood of the faithful, and so to lead them more deeply into the paschal mystery of Christ. Even the cultic aspects of the ministerial priesthood should strive to make the paschal transformation of the people and the exercise of their Christian existence and their baptismal priesthood both possible and easier.

The liturgical texts express Christ's priestly and mediatory role. We say that we do everything through Christ: *"per Christum Dominum nostrum."* We conclude every liturgical prayer with this christological profession of faith.

Although we hold Christ's mediatory role as a dogma of central importance to the liturgy, we should not forget that Jesus Christ is not merely mediator, but also one Person of the Trinity, that is, God himself, towards whom our worship is directed, just as it is directed towards the Father. The Church was always aware that every liturgical prayer should be directed explicitly to the Father. In the third century one of the Synods of Carthage defined this: "Whenever we stand at the altar, we direct always our prayers to the Father" *(Quando ad altare assistitur, semper ad Patrem dirigitur oratio)*. The Father is the beginning and the end, everything is directed towards him. This orientation is found in most of our liturgical texts. Some texts, however, address Christ. These date from the time of the Arian heresy, which saw Christ as only a mediator and denied his divinity. In confronting this heresy, the Church introduced some prayers that address Christ directly as God, thereby indicating that he is not merely a mediator, but God himself. Similar problems also led the Church to change the text of our doxology. In the first three centuries the Christian doxology was: "Glory to the Father through the Son in the Holy Spirit." The Oriental Church uses this doxology up to this day. But when the Arian controversy was rampant, St. Basil the Great introduced another formula: "Glory to the Father and to the Son and to the Holy Spirit," to emphasize that all three divine Persons are God because they all have one and the same divine nature. All three divine Persons therefore deserve to receive *berakah*, that is the praise proper to God.

When we speak about the christological dimension of the liturgy, we must also say something about Christ's liturgical presence. We have already seen that in the liturgy Christ has an active mediatory, priestly, sacrificial role. But, at the same time, Christ the sacrament of God makes the invisible God present to us in a visible way.

How do we understand "presence"? Presence unfolds when two persons are in contact—though not necessarily physical contact—with each other. Presence becomes human, personal presence when some kind of spiritual contact is established between us, a contact of intellect and will that corresponds to our human nature. The depth of relationship between such persons is based on how much they know and love each other. The more I know and love someone, the more I can be present to them. True presence arises, becomes actual, becomes an event, or even enjoyment only if in some real way I come in contact with the other through a medium of communication—a letter, a word, or something else. Presence becomes personal when I become aware of the other, and at the same time the other becomes aware of me, thus establishing a relationship between us.

We can also apply this understanding to Christ's liturgical presence. Christ is present in many ways in the Church and the world. One of the important statements of the Second Vatican Council is that Christ is present not only in the Eucharist, (what we usually call Real Presence), but also when the word of God is proclaimed, when two or three are gathered together in his name, when the Spirit of Christ takes up dwelling place in the hearts of the faithful and the love of Christ motivates them. Christ is present in the person of the priest who presides at the sacramental encounters, and he is also present in those with whom he identifies himself: the sick, children, the poor: "Whatever you do to one of these, you do it to me!" He also said: "Whoever listens to you, listens to me!" In many similar texts in the gospels, the Lord lays down the foundation of his real presence among us.

Let us take an example which shows how Christ is present through Scripture, or better, when we read and meditate on the Scriptures. Matthew 14: 22-33 describes how the disciples have gone out in a boat; a storm comes up and they are afraid. Christ comes to them, walking on the water, and calls Peter to himself. Peter starts to walk on the water, but then, because of his lack of faith, begins to sink. The Lord saves him by taking his hand. We can imagine the scene quite colourfully. But can we say that in it Christ becomes present for us? How can it be that a long-past historical event becomes present now after 2,000 years?

Theologians say that this is possible through *remembrance* (*anamnesis*). But we must be careful, because this remembrance is not merely an intellectual process, such as remembering the 1976 Montreal Olympics. Our concern here is that whenever I meditate on this text or celebrate it liturgically, then I—and we as community—establish contact with the person of Christ. Here are two persons, Christ and I, who know and love one another. I cannot doubt Christ's knowledge and love, because he knows and loves me more than anyone else. Therefore presence between us will be established when, with my own intellect and love, I want to be present to him, and create a personal, intimate relationship with him. This relationship will be established through a mediating link, in this case the gospel account that I read or hear. Two thousand years ago Christ was present and communicated himself to Peter, John, Mary, etc. From the richness of his heart, he gave them something of his life. They accepted and enjoyed it, and became better for it. Two thousand years ago this Christ revealed himself in this way to Peter. Now through the mystery of the resurrection he sits at the right hand of the Father in heaven. He is the risen Lord, no longer bound by time. He lives in eternity: for him everything—past, present, and even future—exists in the present. The gospel event is present to him now just as I am, today. Today, to be as open towards Christ as they were, we must have the attitude of Peter, John, or Mary, because Christ's attitude is the same today as it was two thousand years ago. He wants to give us what he gave them, his life and love, through presence and encounter, according to our circumstances. The text of the Gospel therefore leads us to knowledge: what Christ wanted, what he gave them, he wants to give us now. We call this personal presence and encounter a salvific grace event. It is realized in our prayers, but even more fully in our liturgy which mediates Christ's presence most fully through the community and sacred symbols.

Thus, through remembrance or anamnesis, Christ becomes present for us so that we may celebrate him and enjoy his presence. Ultimately this is the purpose of the liturgy. The liturgy cannot or should not be used for something else. In the past we used to say: "We go to Mass to gain grace," that is, we used the liturgy to increase our spiritual capital of grace. Of course, we receive grace in the liturgy, but we do not celebrate the liturgy for this reason. Today some people say: "We go to Mass to create community." Again, this position uses the liturgy for something else. Liturgy neither has, nor should it have, any further, utilitarian purpose; we should not use it to get something out of it. But the liturgy has deep meaning. In it we enjoy and celebrate the presence of Christ's person and mystery. The purpose of our life is this: to live in God's presence, and celebrate and enjoy him. This is heaven. This is liturgy's primary task: to introduce us into the mystery of Christ, to bring us into contact and enjoyable encounter with him.

Christ's liturgical presence is thus best manifested in the Eucharist, because there Christ is present, not only through the proclamation and reception of the word, not only through the person of the priest and the presence of the Christian community, not only through the faith, hope and love in the hearts of the faithful, but also because he appears to us under the species of the bread and wine in a somatic way, really, substantially, and tangibly. Beyond that, he is present in the Eucharist actively, dynamically, in a priestly way, through the paschal transformation that is the centre of all liturgical actions.

Chapter 5

LITURGY: THE PRIVILEGED PLACE OF THE WORKING OF THE HOLY SPIRIT

In this chapter we want to investigate the role of the Holy Spirit in the liturgy, that is, the pneumatological dimension of the liturgy. The liturgy is the privileged place of the Holy Spirit's operation. Rather than discuss Western theology's neglect of pneumatology, I am simply presenting a summary of the Trinitarian dimension of our salvation.

We speak of the economic Trinity, that is, about how the Trinity is working in our salvation history. The Father, to whom every liturgical prayer is directed through Jesus Christ, is the origin and goal of everything. The Father sends us his Son who becomes man precisely that he may speak to us and relate to us in a human way, and that through this human relationship we may be led back to God. We have also seen that Christ's mission reaches its peak in the four phases of the paschal mystery, with the result that he pours the Holy Spirit into our hearts. Thus, the indwelling of the Holy Spirit brings us into the circle of love that exists between the three divine Persons.

There are two missions in the Trinity. First, the Father sends the Son who becomes man; second, the Father and the Son (or the Father through the Son) send the Holy Spirit who comes to dwell in our hearts and joins us to the life of the Trinity. We should be careful not to separate the two missions. The two missions, the mission of the Son and the mission of the Holy Spirit, are in strict relationship with one another and are directed to each other. It is important to emphasize this, because throughout history one or the other mission has often been overrated to the detriment of the other. There are similar tendencies today. If we accept only the Son's mission, which is manifested in the incarnation, and forget about the Holy Spirit's mission, it would be easy to fall into the extreme, which overemphasizes the continuation of Christ's incarnate reality in the Church, its institutions and organizations, and neglects the intimate, spiritual, pneumatic character of Christian life. When this happens, the Church becomes too institutionalized and forgets about the ultimate goal of the divine mission, spiritual sanctification. If, however, without reference to Christ's incarnation, the mission of the Holy Spirit is overrated, we fall into the other extreme. This has happened in Montanism and Priscillianism and with the Albigensians. Even today we can detect it in the manifestations of an exaggerated charismatic religiosity. These deviations usually do not appreciate Christ's mission, that God comes to us through the Incarnation, and that through the Incarnation the Holy Spirit is poured into us. Since the charismatic movement nowadays plays a rather significant part in the life of the Church, we have to watch that it does not polarize the Church's incarnational and charismatic mission. The two divine missions are always in harmony with one another; they are connected and directed to one another. The Incarnation and Christ's redemptive work, his paschal mystery, are directed to the outpouring of the Holy Spirit, so that through the Holy Spirit, Christ and the Father might come to dwell in our hearts. The Holy Spirit makes the encounter with Christ intimate, and imprints it in our hearts. The operation of the Holy Spirit in our hearts is always directed towards incarnation. The Holy Spirit is never separated from the incarnate Christ, but always aims at an even deeper incarnation of Christ in us and in the Church. The mutual relationship and connectedness of these two missions are very important in understanding salvation-history and the history of the Church, as well as our spiritual life and the liturgy.

Many scripture texts illustrate that the Holy Spirit is always moving towards incarnation. The Incarnation itself is the work of the Holy Spirit: when the Holy Spirit comes upon the Blessed Virgin Mary, she conceives the Christ. The Holy Spirit led Christ in his messianic work. It was through the Holy Spirit that Christ performed his miracles. When Christ was praying, the Holy Spirit inspired him,

Liturgy: The Privileged Place of the Working of the Holy Spirit

and he offered himself on the cross through the Holy Spirit, just as he rose by the power of the Holy Spirit. The Holy Spirit was always present in Christ's life, yet the outpouring of the Spirit is still the result of Christ's redeeming action.

It is the same in the life of the Church. Christian life begins through a human, incarnational, ecclesial, sacramental encounter. Through the proclamation of the word, or through human contacts, we come to believe, we come closer to the Church and to Christ. Gradually we come to the sacramental moment when the Holy Spirit is poured into our hearts in baptism. During our Christian life, the presence of the Holy Spirit continually deepens in us, especially through the sacraments. The primary work of this indwelling Holy Spirit is to configure us to Christ, to conform us to the image of Christ (*homoiosis*), so that we may take on the form of Christ, be clothed in him, become like him. Then the Holy Spirit inspires us to become living, edifying, active members of the Christian community. The Spirit leads us into the community of the Church to build up the Church. The Holy Spirit constantly inspires us to embody our inner spiritual life in words, deeds and service. The Holy Spirit is given to us, not so we can withdraw into ourselves and live apart from the rest of the world, but so that we can reveal and embody our inner selves in the world.

This Trinitarian thesis also applies to the liturgy. Scripture distinguishes two functions of the Holy Spirit: interiorizaton and exteriorization. The Holy Spirit first *interiorizes,* makes things intimate, deepens our spiritual life. The Holy Spirit writes and burns into our hearts everything that we receive through words, human relationships, the teaching of the Church, from Scripture, from our encounter with Christ, This is the characteristic work of the Holy Spirit: to make things spiritual. Perhaps we can understand it better if we realize that it makes little sense to learn the whole Bible by heart, if we do not become saints. The scriptural text that mediates Christ to us, enabling us to encounter God, becomes a living reality only if the fire of the Holy Spirit writes it on our hearts. According to St. John, the Holy Spirit will teach us everything that Jesus taught to us, and will instill in our hearts all that Christ wants from us. How often we read the same scripture text until one day the same text touches our heart and becomes part of our bloodstream! From that moment on, the words sound completely different because they have come alive.

This is the fruit of the Holy Spirit's work. Thus, the first task of the Holy Spirit is interiorization: to make all that we received from Christ our intimate possession, to write it into our hearts. Once the external encounter becomes an inner reality, then exteriorization, the Spirit's other function comes to the foreground. The Holy Spirit leads us to witness: to manifest what lives deep in our hearts. If we have nothing inside, then we cannot manifest anything. So first we need interiorization! Once the Holy Spirit takes up a dwelling-place in us, the same Spirit sends us into the world as witnesses by forming the incarnate Christ in us. He wants to shape our external behaviour according to the image of Christ especially in building up of the Body of Christ, the Christian community, the Church.

If we consider the work of the Holy Spirit in the liturgy, then we find that the Holy Spirit enables us to pray. Romans 8 says that when we do not know how to pray, the Holy Spirit will pray in us. This is so in every kind of prayer. The Holy Spirit is the milieu of our prayer. We could also say, according to the traditional expression of the Church, that we pray "in the Holy Spirit," in communion (*koinonia*) with the Holy Spirit. We pray to the Father through Jesus Christ in the Holy Spirit: *in Spiritu Sancto*. This is how we conclude our liturgical prayers. Thus we say that the Holy Spirit prays in us, and we pray in communion with him.

Few liturgical prayers are directed to the Holy Spirit. Most are directed to the Father, some address Christ, but we have no liturgical prayers to the Holy Spirit except the two medieval hymns *Veni Sancte Spiritus*, and the *Veni Creator Spiritus*. We have private prayers to the Holy Spirit, and it is right to talk to the Holy Spirit, who is a divine person, in our prayers. But our liturgical sense suggests that, in the liturgy, we should pray to the Father through Jesus Christ in the Holy Spirit. Why? Perhaps because although we acknowledge the Divine Person of the Holy Spirit, we have no image of him. We have an image of the Father: the LORD, the almighty God. We have an image of Jesus Christ, who became incarnate precisely that we might have a human image of God. But of the Holy Spirit we have no concrete image, just symbols. That is why we cannot turn to him in a prayer-dialogue, because it is difficult to extrapolate him from our inner self when we pray. He is so united with us, so intimately connected with us, that when we pray, he prays in us. We can hardly

Liturgy: The Privileged Place of the Working of the Holy Spirit

distinguish whether he prays in us or whether we ourselves are praying. We both pray together. This is one of the absolute mysteries of our faith: the mystery of the Holy Spirit, the mystery of Uncreated Grace, the mystery of God's co-operation with the human being. We experience this in our liturgical prayer because, especially there, we pray in the Holy Spirit, inspired by the Holy Spirit, in communion with the Holy Spirit: *in Spiritu Sancto.*

Furthermore, the Holy Spirit gathers the faithful together and makes them a community, a church, so that they may respond to God's word as his people and family. Through his ordained servants, the proclamation of the word of God, especially the sacraments and the whole liturgy, in which Christ becomes present, the Holy Spirit builds up the Church. There we join the mystery of Christ and, through remembrance (*anamnesis*), we enjoy his presence. The working of the Holy Spirit makes Christ's presence and our encounter with him possible.

The Holy Spirit has, therefore, a very important role in the liturgy. We may even say that every single liturgical action is a Pentecost event. In the age of the present charismatic renewal it is good to point this out and become aware that by active participation in the liturgy we truly participate in the Pentecostal event, since the outpouring of the Spirit rounds up the whole paschal mystery.

One of the signs of the presence and operation of the Holy Spirit is exceeding joy (*aggaliasis*). This exceeding joy characterized the early Christian liturgical communities when they professed their faith in the Risen Christ. This exceeding joy will not always be expressed loudly; it may be present even in deep silence. Yet, this genuine joy which is the fruit of the Holy Spirit is a sure sign of the Spirit's presence.

Another sign of the operation of the Holy Spirit in us is an intimate, prayerful attitude. We see this whenever the liturgy becomes, not just an exact performance of external rites, but an intimate, prayerful celebration. It may also happen that occasionally some charismatic gifts do manifest the presence of the Holy Spirit. These are, however, extraordinary phenomena. According to the directives of St. Paul, they too should fit organically into the order of the liturgy. Furthermore, they should always serve the unity of the community and the building up of the Church, not disturb it. The true gifts of the Holy Spirit should be discerned according to this criterion: do they build up the Church or not? The working of the Holy Spirit promotes daily Christian life and service. Wherever liturgical spirituality is incarnated in social service, the Holy Spirit is there.

A special moment of the liturgical operation of the Holy Spirit is the *epiklesis*. This prayer begs the Father to send us the Holy Spirit. Every liturgical action, every sacramental liturgy contains such an *epiklesis*. The *epiklesis* is very important in the liturgy because it expresses that the Church—in spite of the Christ's promises and assurances—always depends on Christ as servants on their master. She never can dispose the gifts of God in an independent way. The Church must always beg for both the coming of the Holy Spirit and the Spirit's gifts. We can never presume them. Although the Church has the consecrative, forgiving, and other powers that guarantee Christ's grace and power, in every liturgical action it must manifest its fundamental dependence, in which it humbly begs and entreats the Father for the gifts of the Holy Spirit. We ought to make the *epiklesis* more solemn and direct everyone's attention to it.

The external sign of the *epiklesis* is normally the imposition of hands, which is connected in every sacramental liturgy with the epicletic prayer. Whether explicit or implicit, the calling down of the Holy Spirit ought to be present in even liturgy. (In the past it has often been simplified or neglected.) We ought to perform the *epiklesis* as we do at ordinations, when the bishop imposes his hands in silence on the head of the ordained, while the whole community intensively and silently begs the Father to send down the Holy Spirit. We could also learn from the East Syrian eucharistic liturgy, in which the priest prostrates himself at the *epiklesis* and begs the Father for the Spirit. Such is the liturgical expression of that inner attitude which entreats the Father to send the Holy Spirit to sanctify us.

Chapter 6

LITURGY: THE PUBLIC WORSHIP OF THE WHOLE CHURCH

This chapter deals with the communal, ecclesial dimension of the liturgy. Liturgy is communal worship, the public worship of the whole Church. We could also say that the whole Church produces the liturgy, though it is also true that the liturgy produces the Church.

The Church produces the liturgy. The whole Church, head and members, Christ and the members of his Mystical Body together mediate between God and humanity. This is done by the whole Church; therefore, everyone who is baptized into Christ takes part in it. Every liturgical action is the work of the *whole* Church, but a *local* church always performs it. Theologically this means that a sacramental action is valid only if it happens with the intention of doing what the Church wants to do. Valid sacramental liturgy always required this *"intentio faciendi quod facit ecclesia."* In other words, we always do liturgy in the name of the whole Church.

Why is this communal, ecclesial character so important in the liturgy? Because God's revelation is directed primarily to the community, not to individuals—to God's chosen people in the Old Testament, and to the Church in the New Testament. The whole community of believers receives God's revelation and, correspondingly, the whole community has to respond. Individuals receive God's gift as members of the community because they *are* members of the community. Our response to God's revelation is faith, and this faith is first the faith of the Church before it becomes personal faith.

The first characteristic of faith is that it is God's gift. This is seen most clearly in regard to infant baptism. Some people object to it because infants cannot yet respond to God's gift, and therefore, they argue, cannot validly receive the sacrament of baptism. However, faith is not merely a personal act, but first of all God's gracious gift which God can give to whomever he wants. Since the infant is a person from the moment of conception, God can communicate his grace and gift to this tiny person, even if the infant cannot respond in any way that would register on our different psychological instruments. God has the sovereign right and ability to give the gift of faith to those who cannot yet respond in a mature way, or in a way that we can perceive.

The second characteristic of faith is that before it becomes personal faith it is the faith of the Church, of the community. Only in the third place we can say that the act of faith is a personal act. Because personal faith presupposes the faith of the Church, we can say that through baptism a child or an adult first becomes a member of the community of the Church and thus appropriates the faith of this community. This also happens in the case of infants, as infants can appropriate faith through their parents. Then it will be necessary for the germ of this faith (*in semine*) to grow into fully mature faith, so that the baptized at one point personally ratify God's gift and the Church's faith, and commit themselves to it with full consciousness. It is important, therefore, in the process of Christian initiation, that those to be baptized undergo a maturation process, because faith needs time to ripen.

The Church, the whole people of God, celebrates the liturgy in which every baptized Christian is called to participate consciously, actively and fruitfully. It is the duty and privilege of every Christian to celebrate the liturgy. To celebrate liturgy means to bless and praise God, to acknowledge him as the only God, Creator and Father, upon whom we depend in every moment of our life; to acknowledge that every creature is basically good; to acknowledge God's gracious providence and to confess that I am not god. This celebratory blessing of God also includes surrendering our lives into God's hands. This is the essence of celebration. Thus we can say that every Christian has the duty to celebrate the liturgy, or to "con-celebrate," to celebrate this communal act together. This is what the Second Vatican

Liturgy: The Public Worship of the Whole Church

Council meant by its repeated emphasis on the active participation of every Christian in the liturgy. External actions manifest our inner participation in the liturgy, whether this be simply our presence at the liturgy, our postures, prayerful responses, singing, processing, etc. Some people could be assigned to specific ministries, such as reading the Scripture, singing the psalm, serving at the altar, helping to distribute holy communion, etc. Included among these celebrants is the priest who, like other Christians, needs that inner, celebratory participation, an interior experience and dedication (*devotio*). (Cf. SC. 11, 14.)

Since the liturgy is the public worship of the whole Church, it follows that every baptized Christian profits from every liturgical celebration. No matter where or how small, the celebration of one community touches every Christian. In general, we celebrate sacramental liturgies at decisive moments of an individual Christian's life. Through the Church God marks the event with his incarnate grace and gives an assurance of his love. Thus, although the sacraments always refer to individuals, both the assembled community and the world-wide Christian community profit from them.

The community's presence at liturgical celebrations is extremely important, because the community is a powerful and effective liturgical symbol that deeply influences the actual grace-encounter between God and the human person. From experience we know what Vatican II clearly states: those liturgical actions at which the community is actively present are much more impressive because their presence expresses tangibly the interest of the whole Church. (Cf. SC. 27.)

Past decades stressed that sacramental liturgy manifested the essence of the Church. Baptism indicates the growth of the Church. In the sacrament of Reconciliation the sinful, yet purified Church appears when God's forgiving grace touches the human person. In the sacrament of Marriage, God's love is present in a tangible way through the mutual love of the couple. Each of the other sacraments shows the nature and essence of the Church as well.

Although the whole Church, that is, every baptized person, participates in liturgical celebrations, the people of God are led in these actions by their appointed ordained leaders. That is, the people of

God, the Church, is hierarchically organized. While this idea may not be very popular today, this hierarchical structure belongs to the essence of the Church. This means that among the people of God some are chosen, ordained or appointed by some other way (such as canonical appointments for parish leadership) to lead the people of God. They have received the vocation to leadership.

There are different functions or ministries, both in the Church and in the liturgy. There is not only the ministry of priests and deacons, but also other ministries as well: lectors, exorcists, catechists, etc. These have arisen within the Christian community because there was a need for them in the community's life. The appointment of these ministers come either from God, or from the ecclesial community. To perform a certain ministry, ministers need a mandate from the church to serve in the name of the church, not just as private persons.

We often hear today that the Church should recognize and establish more ministries in addition to these current ones. During the past centuries, for different reasons, the priestly order absorbed almost all other ministries. Consequently priests became overburdened. They do certain things that others could do just as well, or even better. Therefore it is useful to consider the real task of the priesthood, so that the specific work of other ministries is more clearly established. It is well known that Christian life involves *diakonia*, service. Every baptized Christian has to serve others if he wants to follow Christ who came, not to be served, but to serve. Since we all have been joined to Christ through baptism, we are all called to serve. Honest Christians do this naturally either in their family, or in society.

Beyond this general service there also exists in the Church specialized services that appear in two different categories. First, there are those ministries that emerge from local talent to respond to needs of the local church, or to build up the community. This kind of ministry always existed in the Church, and its re-introduction and acceptance is among the important tasks of the Church today. Unfortunately, we are not yet at the point of recognizing the different types of services among the faithful, or acknowledging as ministers these servants who do their work in the name of the Church. I am thinking here of teachers, social workers, and people who undertake other charitable activities that are not merely volunteer or paid jobs, but also serve the Church in the local community.

The other specialized service in the Church is the ordained ministry, with its own sacrament. The sacrament of Holy Orders has three degrees: episcopacy, presbyterate (priesthood) and diaconate. Neither temporary nor optional, this special ministry does not depend on local needs or talents. It belongs to the Church's structure, its permanent and constitutional essence, and makes the Church a hierarchical organization. This group of people has been called by God to be leaders of the community. We will not understand the nature of this ministry completely if we rely only on the texts of the Council of Trent, which, rooted in the polemics of the sixteenth century, consider the ordained priesthood in a somewhat restricted way. From the beginning of the second millennium, priesthood was considered almost exclusively in its relationship to the Eucharist, to the performance of cultic actions, and its activity was restricted to the sanctuary and the consecration.

We should look for the roots of ordained ministry in the College of the Apostles. Perhaps it would be even better to call this priesthood "apostolic ministry," that is, a ministry entrusted by Christ to the Apostles which they handed on to chosen persons through the laying on of hands and the epicletic prayer of ordination. Thus, rooted in the Apostolic College, this "order" has the task of continuing the ministry of the Apostles: to spread the kingdom of God, proclaim the word of God, establish local communities, and so build up the Church in every part of the earth until the end of the world. Whenever, therefore, we consider the priestly office and look for its origin in Scripture, it is not enough simply to point to the text of the Last Supper when the Lord Jesus said to the Apostles: "Do this in memory of me!" We find a much richer source in the ministry of the apostles themselves. We will investigate these roots following the reflection of Raymond Brown.

One biblical image of the apostolic ministry is the shepherd. The texts of the Old and New Testament beautifully describe the role of the Good Shepherd whose task is to lead the flock, feed it, and defend it from every danger.

Another image is the servant or deacon who is called to serve his master. He is not the lord, but the servant who always performs his work in the name of his lord. The servant does not demand special privileges for himself; he lives for others. Another image, the Rock, refers not just to Peter, but also to the other apostles, the solid foundation-stones, sustaining pillars, upon whom we build, and from whom we receive strength and encouragement.

Perhaps the most important characteristic of the apostolic ministry is that the apostles have first been disciples of the Lord Jesus. From among his disciples the Lord chose the twelve apostles. In other words, to become an apostle, one has to be a disciple first. To be a disciple means to be close to the Master, sitting at his feet and listening to his every word. Disciples are with their Master day and night; they try to guess the Master's thoughts and listen to his heartbeat. Closeness to the person of Jesus Christ makes someone an apt subject to be chosen as an apostle and represent the Lord to others. This intimate friendship with the Master characterizes true disciples. From these friends the Lord can demand what he does not want to ask from others: that they follow him in poverty and obedience, leave behind their family, or follow him to the cross. This apostolic ministry, which is the essence of the priestly order, is based on the relationship between the Master and his disciple. The call (vocation) that invites us to this ministry invites us first to the personal service of Christ, and only then to serve the flock. Priests must therefore be disciples first; they have to spend time at the Master's feet and establish an intimate relationship with him, so that they can represent him to the flock. This personal relationship to Christ is the essence of the priestly, apostolic ministry.

Another biblical image of priestly ministry is the apostle. An apostle is someone whom the Lord has chosen among his disciples and sends into the world as his personal ambassador and representative. Apostles thus signify the Lord's personal presence, making the Lord present in their own person. Here is the sacramental root of the priestly order. The ordained priest, a sacramental representative making present Jesus Christ, is a living sacramental symbol. Through his person, no matter how weak his human nature, Christ becomes present. Priests are chosen to make Christ present in their person, anywhere in the world, under any circumstances.

This apostolic mission includes many functions; of first importance is the proclamation of the Good News in the form of kerygma, teaching, or homily. It includes the celebration of the sacraments, counselling and consoling, caring for the sick and the poor, and fostering different forms of human relationships. The apostolic work can also include daily chores to which St. Paul himself attests: work by which we earn our daily bread, manual work, such as sweeping and cleaning the church, or doing other chores around the house. Included in the work of the apostle is collecting money for the poor, as did St. Paul when he collected money for the faithful of Jerusalem. There is also the apostleship of prayer, when before the Blessed Sacrament, or in the silence of their room, priests beg the Lord on behalf of their people. Nor should we forget the apostleship of suffering in which we all share either through sickness, old age, failure or spiritual sufferings. Inescapable, these are all part of our apostolic ministry.

Finally, at the root of priestly ministry is the image of the presbyter and the bishop to whom the leadership of a local church has been entrusted. Their task is to build up the ecclesial community. Here, finally, we come to the eucharistic role of the priest. The apostolic ministry obliges the priest to lead and feed the community and, especially, to help the people of God live and practice their Christian vocation, their existential priesthood. The ordained priest makes it possible for them to celebrate the Eucharist so they can experience this paschal mystery sacramentally. The priest has to lead his people to this summit of Christian life by many kinds of pastoral and apostolic works. Because the Eucharist is the source, centre and summit of the whole priestly, apostolic ministry, we can say that it is the heart of priestly life. But it is not everything. Priestly service must not be restricted to cultic actions, as if the priest had nothing else to do than to say Mass on Sunday or even daily.

This demands a better understanding of the difference between the priesthood of the faithful and the ordained priesthood. All the baptized, including the priest, are obliged to practise their existential priesthood, to offer their lives as sacrifice in the Eucharist, and surrender themselves to the Father. This existential sacrifice is more important than cultic priestly service. On the other hand, the purpose of our election to priestly ministry is to stand before the faithful, gather them around the altar and make possible for them the celebration of the paschal mystery in the Eucharist.

The priest's explicitly "priestly" role, as Apostolic Minister, consists in offering the liturgical, sacramental sacrifice. He is called "priest" (*sacerdos*) because he ritually offers sacrifice. In the first century the apostles and their immediate successors were not yet called priests, because the office of priest was at that time connected with Old Testament temple sacrifices. Christian priests wanted to distinguish themselves from Old Testament priests; therefore, the language of priesthood was used only when the Temple of Jerusalem and its priesthood did not exist anymore. Thus by the second century, the leaders of the Christian community, the bishops and presbyters were able to be called priests. At the same time, Christians began to realize that the Eucharist is the sacrifice of the New Testament, the making-present of Christ's sacrifice on the cross. Consequently they began to call those who led the eucharistic celebrations and performed the ritual "priests." This is the role of the ministerial priesthood in the Church: their ordination enables them to lead the liturgy in which the faithful join by their active participation.

In connection with the ecclesial character of liturgy we should point out, that in the episcopally structured churches (such as the Catholic, Anglican, and Orthodox Churches) the bishop is the symbol, guarantor and custodian of unity and fidelity—of orthodoxy. The bishop's duty is to direct the liturgy. In the local church (diocese), it is the bishop's responsibility and right to lead the liturgy. Priests, the bishop's helpers, make Christ present through their ordination as apostolic ministers, but at the same time they also represent the bishop in the diocese. If we want to claim that our liturgy is truly the liturgy of the whole Church, that is, an authentic "catholic" liturgy, then everything must happen with the knowledge and approval of the bishop, that is, in communion (*koinonia*) with the bishop. This is why we profess our union with the bishop in every eucharistic liturgy by mentioning his name. This is an important part of our liturgy because the local parish or small community in itself is not yet the Church. It will become an organic part of the whole, universal, catholic Church, if the union, the communion, the *koinonia* with the bishop is assured. The bishop, of course, has to be in union with the other bishops and with the whole Episcopal College, together with its head, the Bishop of Rome. The ancient Christian character of this *koinonia* belongs to the essence of the Church, because union around the eucharistic altar best manifests what the Christian community is about. Liturgy is always celebrated concretely by a local church, but this local church must be in communion with the other local churches through the ministry of the priests and the bishop.

This concept of koinonia is very important in the liturgy. Already in the second century St. Ignatius of Antioch emphasized that without the bishop's consent neither baptism, nor Eucharist is valid. In other words, a maverick, freelancing priest could not perform the liturgy validly (except in cases described by Canon Law, such as absolving in danger of death). A priest who is not in communion with the bishop cannot practice his priestly ministry. This is clearly expressed in connection with the sacrament of Penance: to absolve validly, the priest needs faculties or jurisdiction (a canonical term). Both simply indicate that the priest is in communion with the bishop. This communion is also required for celebrating the other sacraments.

What about the axiom "The liturgy produces the Church"? The word of God calls the people together, and through their response of faith, the faithful become God's family, community, church. Whenever God communicates to us his love and life, this divine grace always leads to the formation of a community, to which we are invited to belong. On the other hand, the opposite of grace, sin, always breaks up community.

Liturgy produces a church that is one, holy, catholic, and apostolic. True liturgy builds up unity, because it forges the community into one. True liturgy produces a holy church, because it makes the community holy. It makes the community catholic, or universal, by imbuing it with a missionary spirit that is poured out to every part of the world, desiring to penetrate everything. Finally, it makes the community apostolic, in that it preserves contact with the Apostles by keeping the apostolic doctrine intact, celebrating the apostolic liturgy and helping to realize the apostolic lifestyle. All of these are guaranteed by the apostolic ministry.

Most of this build-up of the Church happens through the liturgy. It begins with baptism and continues with the other sacraments, especially with the Eucharist celebrated regularly, so that the body of Christ may become more and more complete.

There are practical conclusions to be drawn from the communal, ecclesial character of the liturgy. Since the liturgy is the public worship of the whole Church, liturgical prayer always speaks in the plural. Liturgical prayer is always in the plural, because it is said in the name of the whole Church. Private prayers have no place in liturgical texts. Private prayers contained in the liturgical books are all for private use, for the priest's private devotion or that of others, and should therefore be said in silence.

Our liturgies must be open. They should not become exclusive, secret, sectarian gatherings. Small communities—base communities—which are very important, must watch that they remain open, that they do not become sects limited to select members. Since small communities have an important role to play in the Church of today and tomorrow, we should pay more attention to the adaptation of our celebrations to their circumstances. Small communities need to maintain their relationship with the parish or diocesan communities, which should lead the small community towards them. Larger parish communities should occasionally experience a more intimate setting for liturgy, which can promote deeper participation.

On certain occasions a particular group may come together to celebrate the liturgy, but it should never become so esoteric that it excludes others. Liturgy—particularly Sunday Eucharist— belongs to all Christians, and every baptized Christian has a right to take part in it.

The style of our liturgical celebrations, be they in a small or a large community, should be adapted to the group's sociological makeup and its size. The appropriate liturgical room (small chapel, parish church, or large cathedral church), and the appropriate environment greatly contribute to a good celebration of the liturgy.

As a communal, ecclesial action, liturgy has a certain, defined structure. This structure is laid down in the liturgical books, so everyone can know ahead of time what to expect. There should be no surprises. Liturgy does not allow sudden individual spiritual manifestations by priest or lay person. Because the priest does not celebrate his own liturgy, but the Church's, he may not impose his own idiosyncrasies on others.

Chapter 7

LITURGY: PERFORMED IN THE WORLD OF SYMBOLS

Liturgy speaks the language of symbols that human beings can perceive. Similarly our faith-response is expressed in signs. This is what we mean when we say that the twofold communication of the liturgy happens in the world of symbols. The sacramental encounter is surrounded by these liturgical signs, through which we encounter the mystery of Christ.

Every sacrament is surrounded by liturgical signs which deepen and make more intimate the encounter with God and with Christ. While most liturgical symbols (except those that form the matter and form of the sacraments) normally do not belong to the essence of the liturgy, they constitute the milieu of the sacramental encounter, and as such play an important role in the process. Unfortunately, in celebrating the sacraments in the past, we paid attention only to those things that were absolutely necessary for the valid conferral of the sacraments, i.e., the matter and form. We thought that if the pouring of the water, accompanied by certain words, happened, then baptism had been conferred. We failed to take into account the other signs and symbols of the rite of baptism.

Today many people have lost their sense of symbol. Therefore we ought to try to reawaken this sensitivity in both children and adults. The meaning of these signs comes either from Christ or the Church, and therefore we ought to learn their origin, history and development, so they are meaningful to us. That is why the history of liturgy is so important. It is not necessary, however, to explain the liturgical signs every time, or comment on them one by one. Catechesis enables people to grow into the symbolic world of the liturgy from childhood, so that this world constitutes the matrix of our religious experiences, just as the carols of Christmas evoke and create the symbolic world of Christmas.

Every sacramental symbol and liturgical sign has three dimensions. The first looks to the past *(signum rememorativum)*. On seeing the symbol, we remember the past and investigate its scriptural origin in the Old or New Testament. An immense treasure opens up for us when we recognize the typological and other meaning of the symbols, which the Fathers of the Church used with great profit. The symbol enables us to call to mind the events of salvation history related to it. Such remembering enriches the basic content of the symbol. We also discover that over the two thousand years of the Church's history the spirituality of Christian people has always added meaning and content to these signs. This process indicates the importance of tradition because these symbols carry two thousand years of religious experience. Thus, every liturgical symbol reminds us of the past.

Secondly, liturgical symbols also make present the grace that God has already communicated to us in the past, and that he now wants to give us anew through these symbols. The liturgical symbol expresses God's gift now in a sensible way *(signum demonstrativum)*. The communication of grace happens effectively through these sacramental signs and other liturgical symbols.

The third aspect of liturgical symbols is directed to the future *(signum prognosticum)*. Already it indicates the coming fulfillment. Just as every sacrament reaches its perfect fulfillment only in the future, in the eschaton, so do liturgical symbols find their fulfillment only in the future, for only in heaven will we truly perceive and understand their meaning.

One of the most important liturgical signs of both the past and the present is the community, because it seems that the experience of the Sacred is best communicated to modern people through community. One category of liturgical symbols is liturgical persons, such as the person of the priest, who is the living sacramental sign of Christ's presence. In the liturgy the priest is called to express not just his own identity, but also something else: the presence of Christ. For this reason he wears a distinguishing vestment during the liturgical action. Liturgical prayers, texts, songs, music, that is, everything that expresses through words our response of faith to God, forms another group of liturgical symbols. Other categories of liturgical symbols include liturgical actions, gestures, postures, rites and rituals; there are also liturgical objects, vessels, images, statues; there are liturgical places, churches, chapels, and their furnishings; and finally there is the liturgical time, or liturgical year, through which we are immersed in the rhythm of the Church, which from day to day, week to week, season to season makes present to us the mystery of Christ.

Classical theology taught that the sacraments and the liturgy communicate God's grace to us by signifying the inner content of the signs, that is, God's grace *(significando causant gratiam)*. Thus, unless we can perceive the meaning of the signs, they cannot communicate grace. Therefore these signs must be more complete and more understandable. Understanding, however, does not mean rational, intellectual perception, as if we ought to meditate each time on the significance of the signs. Symbols work by constituting the milieu of our life and our inner world. To be able to respond to them, we need to be able to grasp their significance.

Theology also teaches that the sacraments work *"ex opere operato,"* which essentially means that Christ gives us grace. In other words, we encounter Christ in the sacraments. However, the perception and acceptance of liturgical symbols are neither superfluous nor negligible. No sacrament arises without some kind of reception on the part of the recipient *(ex opere operantis)*. The more people can perceive and understand sacramental and liturgical symbols, the better the possibility for a deeper encounter with Christ. Since liturgical signs play such an important role in grace encounters, we must reject the liturgical minimalism that wants to restrict the rite to the "essential" sacramental form and, as far as possible, exploit the richness of liturgical signs.

Some people criticize liturgical symbols as difficult to understand in today's technological society. While it is true that people's lives today are not surrounded by the symbols of nature or those of a nomadic or agrarian society, we can re-introduce them to common awareness. As far as possible, we should strive to make these signs rich to mediate their content to our contemporaries. The potential of liturgical symbols is immense.

Chapter 8

LITURGY: DIALOGUE IN WORDS

(Liturgy of the Word)

The Second Vatican Council explicitly stated that the proclamation of the word of God should occupy a more significant place in our liturgy (SC. 24, 35). Prior to Vatican II every liturgy included two scripture readings, and the liturgical texts (prayers, antiphons, etc.) were also largely taken from scripture texts.

Yet, there is no doubt that the liturgy of the word had retreated to a subordinate role throughout the centuries. In the first Christian centuries Christians had gathered together daily, morning and evening, to bless and praise God, and listen to his word. Through their teaching, the Fathers of the Church led the people into the mysteries of the word.

The liturgy of the word originated in Jewish tradition. Jesus Christ participated in the liturgy of the synagogue; the apostles, especially St. Paul, all taught in the synagogues and proclaimed the word there. Christians continued this worship tradition. The liturgy of the word always preceded the celebration of the sacraments. This liturgy, therefore, comes not from the sixteenth century Protestant reform, but from the earliest Christian forms of worship. In both the Old Testament and the New, God's word calls the people of God into a community, into a "Church" whose fundamental task is to listen to and proclaim the word of God. This does not just refer to our missionary task of preaching the word to those who have not heard it, but to a genuine liturgy in which the faithful encounter God just as truly as in the sacramental liturgies and the Eucharist. In the liturgy of the word we encounter the Holy God. Here too we bless and praise the Creator and Covenant God, confess our nothingness and surrender ourselves into God's hands. In the liturgy of the word, too, Christ speaks, and we enjoy his presence through the words of Holy Scripture. Like the other sacraments, the liturgy of the word is also a grace-communicating event. The word of God is the sacramental sign. And just as the other sacraments have external, material and vocal signs, so the word of God is such a sign—an audible, perceptible reality—in which God communicates through living words what he wants to give us. The external, audible sound of the word contains and hides within itself an invisible reality that is nothing other than the grace, love and life that God wants to give us through our listening to the word. The liturgical and quasi-sacramental character of the liturgy of the word is a grace encounter.

Liturgy presupposes external structure and symbols. Not every form of reading of scripture is a liturgy of the word. Certain external and structural conditions are needed to make it a liturgy. First, the liturgy of the word should be universal, that is, catholic. It should not be just the prayer of an individual or a small group, no matter how laudable and necessary these might be. Whenever we celebrate liturgy we are acting in the name of the whole Church. We listen to the word of God in the name of the whole Church; we receive God's message and self-communication in the name of the whole Church, and we give our faith response, our profession of faith in the name of the whole Church. Thus the whole church benefits from our grace encounter with Christ, which makes our liturgy universal, that is, catholic.

Second, we have to pay attention to the fact that the liturgical celebration of the word is always a dialogue. God's word comes to us from above: from God, from Christ, from the Church. Through the lector's reading of scripture it comes to us listeners. When the Holy Spirit inspires us to respond, the response comes from below. We need to help contemporary people, ourselves included, learn how to listen to the word of God fruitfully, since in the noise of today's world we can forget how to do this. Without true listening, the word of God can penetrate our hearts only with great difficulty, there to elicit religious experiences which we can then express in our responses. We need to become aware of Christ's presence in the liturgy of the word, because only in this way can we establish contact with him, open ourselves to him and receive his gifts. Since Christ is at work in the proclamation of the word of God, it is efficacious, even if it is not connected with any other sacrament.

Third is the use of liturgical symbols. These symbols may vary according to the circumstances, but they have to be present and expressed in some form if we want to have liturgy, and not just a prayer meeting. The Book of the Gospels and the Lectionary are liturgical symbols. Their appearance and how we treat them should mediate for us the presence of Christ. In the Oriental liturgy, the Book of the Gospel is decorated with precious pearls and small icons and carried around in solemn procession. The Book of the Gospels is placed on the altar; the Lectionary, on the ambo. The way we handle the Bible itself may already betray our relationship to it: we do not carry it under our arm, but raise it high as something very precious. Showing the Scriptures, venerating them with kisses, incensing and surrounding the book with candles and placing flowers in front of the ambo all call our attention to the importance of the word and to Christ's presence in it. Our posture also helps create the proper milieu for listening to the word. When we listen to it, we sit, except during the reading of the gospel, when we express our veneration of the mystery of Christ by standing. Readers (lectors) represent Christ and the Church in their persons, and proclaim the word in the name of Christ and the Church. Therefore it is fitting that they stand to read, indicating that this is an important message that comes from above.

In the strict sense we cannot call it "liturgy" of the word when two or three of us come together to read the Bible and discuss it, and perhaps pray about it. The prayer meetings of the charismatic communities, where participants meditate completely freely on the Scriptures, and pray about them, and perhaps share their faith experiences, cannot be called liturgies.

The structure of the liturgy of the word is simple and can be used in all kinds of different circumstances. Its simple and elastic structure consists of the following parts:

1) After the customary greeting and introductory words we briefly confess how small and unworthy we are before God. Then in the opening prayer, we ask the Lord's help for this celebration.

2) One, two or three scriptural readings may follow. These are always accompanied by corresponding answers that express the dialogue between God and humanity. God's word comes to us from above, while the response, in the form of a psalm or canticle comes from below.

3) The homily follows. More will be said about this later.

4) The prayer of the faithful (*Oratio universalis*) follows the homily. Re-introduced into our liturgy with the reform of Vatican II, it revives an ancient Christian custom. The Prayer of the Faithful is an essential part of every liturgy of the word, because in it the people of God, called together by the word of God, pray as one family for the universal needs of the Church, and for the whole human race.

5) The liturgy of the word normally concludes with a blessing and dismissal.

There are many occasions for celebrating a liturgy of the word. Each of the sacraments is celebrated in the context of the liturgy of the word. In addition, there is the funeral vigil service.

The *Order of Christian Funerals* includes three stations: first, the vigil service, which is essentially a liturgy of the word; second, the Funeral Mass; third, the farewell at the grave. The *Order of Christian Funerals* offers several models for liturgies of the word for the vigil. This is the most appropriate form of celebration since many Christians of varied traditions usually attend it, along with people of little religious background. They may well be touched by the word of God on these occasions.

Another opportunity for a liturgy of the word is the exposition or adoration of the Blessed Sacrament. According to the new liturgical directives contained in *Holy Communion and Worship of the Eucharist outside Mass*, exposition ought to be connected with the liturgy of the word. The reading of scripture passages may be followed by a brief homily. A longer period of silent adoration, common prayer for the needs of the universal Church, the solemn recitation of the Lord's

Prayer and benediction, which closes the liturgy of the word, follow.

The communal recitation of the rosary is also a good occasion for a liturgy of the word. Each mystery can be introduced by a scripture text, followed by a brief meditation (homily or appropriate thoughts), and the recitation of a decade of Hail Marys. A similar model is possible with the stations of the cross.

We can also celebrate a liturgy of the word on occasions of family visits and family feasts. Birthdays, wedding anniversaries, and other joyful or sorrowful family events can always be connected with a liturgy of the word, and be occasions to encounter Christ among us. We can fruitfully celebrate the liturgy of the word when we deal with children or youth groups—that is, with people who may not yet be mature enough to celebrate the Eucharist consciously and with full participation. The liturgy of the word offers a good opportunity to introduce them into the mystery of the presence of Jesus Christ. The Roman Ritual also includes different blessings, such as a blessing of a house, blessing of persons, etc. All of these can and should happen within the framework of a liturgy of the word. Extending the liturgy of the word to many occasions would better prepare us to appreciate and enjoy the grace-encounter with Christ.

The reading or rather proclamation of the word has its own special tone. It is neither a monotonous recitation nor a theatrical production, but a proclamation of a sacred text. Whoever reads the biblical text, be they priest, deacon, or lector, should be aware of the honourable service they are undertaking. Such persons should be well prepared so that the proclaimed text can be heard well and understood. Today microphones can carry the voice to everyone. Keep in mind that the liturgy of the word is a dialogue. It is not quite liturgically right, though often it is unavoidable, to read the response from the same place from which the word of God was proclaimed. As far as possible the different readings should be distributed among several readers: if three readings, then three readers—the third always a deacon or priest. The psalm should be sung or read by someone else, with the people responding. Including the people in the dialogue between God and humanity is very important: what happens here is everyone's business, and all should participate both externally, as well as internally.

The prayer of the faithful is an integral part of the liturgy of the word. We call it the universal prayer *(oratio universalis),* because its purpose is universal, embracing everyone and everything. After God's word has gathered us together and forged us into a community, we pray in the name of the whole Church for the whole Church and the whole human race. The petitions should be divided into four categories: (1) the needs of the universal Church; (2) the problems of the world today; (3) the cause of the poor, oppressed and sick; (4) the everyday life of the local church. We should be careful not to let local concerns and individual petitions overwhelm the prayer. In this prayer we ask something from God; we do not praise or give thanks, but simply present our needs to the Father as his children. These petitions ought to be well-prepared each time so that they reflect the actual situation of the church and the world. The people often prepare these prayers of the faithful for each Sunday. In small groups the presider can ask people to present their own intentions.

The prayer of the faithful should always be introduced by the priest, who concludes it with a "collect." If the priest notices that the spontaneous petitions do not satisfy the universal character of the prayer of the faithful, then he should complement them with some universal intentions.

It is important that we keep silence at certain points in the liturgy of the word: after the presider invites us to silent, individual prayer with the call "Let us pray"; after the proclamation of the scriptural texts. If we truly want to promote the grace encounter, then after each reading we should keep silence for at least half a minute. But we first must learn how to use these silences fruitfully, lest they become an empty vacuum. The liturgical silence should let the text we have just heard penetrate our hearts so we can perceive what God wants to give us through these words. After such silence the response will truly arise from our heart.

Now a few words about the homily. The Second Vatican Council indicates that the homily belongs organically to the liturgy (SC. 35). It is prescribed for the Sunday Masses, and is highly recommended at other liturgical celebrations. The Council understands a homily as that kind of exposition of the scriptural text that brings its meaning closer to the people and applies it to their life. Three forms of preaching can be distinguished: kerygma, catechesis, and the homily. Kerygma communicates the message of God in a startling way to a non-believing audience, just as St. Paul and the other Apostles did when they proclaimed that Jesus of Nazareth is the Son of God, who suffered for us, died, rose from the dead and brought us new life. This is kerygma: it shakes people up, shocks them like a lightning bolt and calls them to conversion. We also call it missionary preaching, because it proclaims the Good News that God loves us, and out of love sent his Son to redeem us from the power of darkness. This Christ continues to live among us, enabling us to conquer darkness and sin, and so arrive at eternal life. This is the Good News, the Gospel, the message of salvation. The Church's mission is to proclaim this message to the whole world. Thus, the proper place for kerygma can be any area of life where people long for the light and message of Christ.

The second form of preaching is catechesis, or teaching. Characteristically it is directed to believers who would like to know more about their faith. Catechesis systematically sets out its material day after day, week after week, year after year in a systematic way, according to the theses of dogmatics or moral theology.

Such catechetical instruction properly takes place in the classroom, the school. The style of instruction is calm, rational, systematic, in contrast to the kerygma which wants to touch the hearts of people perhaps even with a thunderbolt, since it wants to convert them. Catechesis speaks to people's intellect to increase and deepen their knowledge of the faith.

The third form of preaching is the homily. The homily is directed to people who have been converted and who already live their Christian life. They come day after day, week after week to celebrate the liturgy and experience and enjoy in it Christ's mysterious presence. They listen to the word of God and respond liturgically as they penetrate more deeply the sacred mysteries of faith and strengthen their Christian identity so that it also permeates their everyday life. The homily is neither kerygma, which tries to convert people, nor catechesis, because its aim is not primarily to teach. Rather it strives to help people be aware of Christ's presence in the scripture and sacramental actions and awaken in them the joyful knowledge that they constitute his

Mystical Body. They are in communion with him, the Holy Trinity dwells in them. How wonderful it is to be a Christian!

The homily should not be used for moral teaching or exhortation. Unfortunately, since the Enlightenment, preaching for the most part had been moralizing. We searched the sacred texts for moral rules and our sermons tried to persuade people to practise virtue and avoid sin. The aim of the homily, in contrast, is to rejoice in the mystery of Christ, enter into it, and be strengthened in our Christian identity. Moral consequences come after all these experiences. A homilist can talk about how can we live out our Christian identity in everyday life as an appendix to the homily, not as its main purpose. This was Saint Paul's method: almost all of his letters can be considered as liturgical homilies. Paul begins his epistles by presenting a heavy dogmatic thesis: Do you know that you are the children of God? Do you know you are a member of the Body of Christ? Do you know that you are the temple of the Holy Spirit? Then he explains in detail what a wonderful reality this is. In this way he invites everyone to share in the joy of being Christian. Later, towards the end of his letters, he may point out some consequences of a truth: for example, if you are the temple of the Holy Spirit, be careful not to desecrate that temple. While it is not easy to reach the primary goal of the homily, it is not as difficult as it may seem. It presupposes that we have an experience of God and of Christ in connection with the scriptural text. If we have this, then we can more easily communicate it to others, so that they too may participate in the gift of grace that comes to us through the scriptural text and the homily.

In pastoral practice this ideal of the homily may encounter many difficulties. Many people are poorly catechized, others, indifferent, and still others live their Christian life faithfully. We ought to direct our homilies towards this latter group; the others are more in need of kerygma or catechesis. An occasional use of the homily for catechesis or preaching is unavoidable. Yet, it is worthwhile to keep the primary goal of the homily before our eyes. Even if the emphasis of a homily is catechesis or kerygma, preachers always should have as their intention to deepen the experience of encountering the mystery through the word of God and the homily.

An ancient and privileged form of the liturgy of the word is the Liturgy of the Hours. Since Vatican II, the church has highly recommended this precious treasure not only for priests and religious, but also for the lay faithful. We call this prayer "Holy Office" (*Officium sanctum*) because it best expresses that praise of God by creation which is the primary task (*officium*) of all creatures. We also call it the "Prayer of the Church" because in it the whole Church prays. It is also "Liturgy of the Hours" (*Liturgia Horarum*) because it is designed to sanctify every hour of the day. At every hour of the day—morning, daytime, evening, and even at night—somewhere in the world we can hear the song of God's praise, sometimes by special choirs, more often from the lips of tired people, who pour out their hearts to the Lord in song. This is the prayer of the Church, born of the spirituality of many centuries. Here we find the whole theology of prayer: praise of God, thanksgiving, petition. It is a true liturgy, characterized by the dialogue between God and humanity; we listen to the word of God in the scriptures, respond to them with hymns and psalms, and beg for the needs of the Church and the whole human race. It is always desirable to celebrate the liturgy of the hours as a true liturgy, rather than just pray it silently in the privacy of our home. Whenever possible, we should celebrate it in common, even if there are only two of us. We could even try to sing some part of it. Perhaps it is not so utopian to sometimes celebrate it more solemnly with the people. I know that some families have adopted the practice of praying the liturgy of the hours together.

Recently some people have objected that the liturgy of the hours (*Breviarium*) is a prescribed, structured prayer, while true prayer should arise spontaneously from our heart and not be forced into certain forms. It is true that spontaneous prayer has much to recommend it, but this form of prayer belongs in the silence of our rooms. The century-long wisdom of the Church has recognized that our frail human nature needs the discipline and regularity of prayer. We ought to pray not only when it pleases us, or when we like it, but we should praise God always, unceasingly (*sine intermissione*) because we have been created for this purpose. In other words, prayer should not depend upon our whims. That is why we call it holy office, sacred obligation! Prayer is the lifeblood not only of priests and religious, but of every believer, and when we do not know how we should pray, the

Holy Spirit teaches us how through the liturgy of the hours. Recently some religious communities have experimented with other forms of liturgical prayer, but after many experiments finally concluded that none of them could surpass the Prayer of the Church in beauty and richness. This little book calls us each day to enter into dialogue with God. Other prayers and devotions may easily satisfy our spiritual hunger, but in this prayer we pray with and for the Church. This prayer is not primarily for our own personal benefit; rather it joins individuals to the great choir of the world-wide Church. We pray, not for ourselves, but for others, and in place of others, for those who do not have time to pray, or for those who most need the healing power of prayer.

Some people complain that the prescribed texts in the liturgy of the hours often do not correspond to their present spiritual mood: if they're sad or dejected, they don't want to sing a joyful hymn. Once again, the wisdom of the Church appears. The prescribed liturgical texts pull us out of our individual isolation and make us realize that even in sadness and spiritual dark nights we have reason to sing Alleluia. On the other hand in joyful moments it is good to admit our weaknesses. The liturgy of the hours offers us a balanced spirituality. We may now be ready to rejoice, but by praying the *Miserere* we speak in the name of those who, right now, badly need that prayer for mercy. If spiritual dryness dominates our souls, we can still praise God joyfully because this best fits on the lips of those for whom we pray. This prayer is the prayer of the Church; we are merely the privileged, appointed representative of the great community of the faithful.

The liturgy of the hours is also important because, as a school of prayer, it contains the whole of revelation and our whole spirituality. It also teaches us how to pray in private. The liturgy of the hours presents to us all the books of the Bible, not just those we like or favour. It does not omit certain passages which may make us uncomfortable because they call us to conversion. Its scriptural texts provide us with daily spiritual food; the peak moments in the liturgy are these biblical texts. The psalms that respond prayerfully to these texts were inspired by the Holy Spirit.

Knowledge of the psalms is essential to properly pray and celebrate the liturgy. Developing a culture of the psalms, which many of our ancestors possessed, is a significant task. First, we must pray and meditate on the psalms privately before we come to sing them in the liturgy. To sing them, we need to become familiar with simple, easily learned psalm-melodies, and then we would only need a text indicating the proper cadences and flexions. The psalms are simple, heart-felt prayers, full of emotions, images and metaphors that lead us to contemplation. Single words or lines may deeply penetrate the mind and heart, so that when we recite them or hear them in the liturgy, our previous spiritual experiences are revived in our soul.

We should also study the psalms, if necessary, with the help of commentaries to learn who wrote the text and under what circumstances. Then we can try to capture the author's spiritual mood and say the words with him. We may recall some event in our own lives when these words should have been on our lips, or pray the psalms in the name of those people, with those who could now truly sing Alleluia or cry Miserere. Almost half of the psalms are songs of praise (*berakah*) that joyfully recognize God's majesty, uniqueness, holiness and goodness, and give thanks for God's manifold benefits (*magnalia Dei*), for life, for the beauty of creation and for everything that comes from God's hand. The other half of the psalms are lamentations, prayers uttered by the lips of a poor, sick or sinful person who has no other hope, and therefore expects everything from God. Thus the fundamental character of our spiritual life becomes manifest in the simple prayers of the psalms.

The intercessions of the liturgy of the hours are similar to the universal prayer of the Mass: we pray to the Father for everyone. Here we can include all those who asked for our prayers and with whom we are joined in Christ Jesus. The Lord's Prayer, the family prayer of the Church, concludes this universal prayer. (Cf. GILH. 179-193.)

Chapter 9

LITURGY: A PROCESS IN THREE PHASES

Liturgy is a process, not just a momentary event. Often we think of the liturgy as a punctual action, when at a certain moment, the sacramental matter and form are applied like lightning from above, and God's grace falls on the recipients. This is not so. Certainly, the Church did not think this way about sacramental events in the first thousand years. Rather, sacramental liturgy is a process in which we can distinguish three phases: preparing for the sacrament, celebrating the liturgy of the sacrament, and living out the sacrament in everyday life. Preparation may last for years, as in the case of the catechumenate, or preparation for the sacrament of Holy Orders. Preparation for the sacrament of marriage varies in length. If preparation is normally a long period, follow-up is even longer, because our whole Christian life is based upon the sacraments of initiation. Marriage and Holy Orders are also characterized by long follow-up periods. The command, "Go in the peace of Christ ..." does not mean that we forget all that happened at the liturgy. Having experienced the summit and the source, Christians now must live from this fountain for the rest of the day, the next week, month, years—a whole lifetime. It follows that the priest's sacramental service not only obliges him to perform the celebration validly, but also to assist people in living out their sacramental life. Far from being a cultic priesthood restricted to the sanctuary, this approach to ministry indicates that priesthood embraces the whole pastoral, and apostolic ministry, because priestly service can be arranged around the sacraments.

Such a view of the sacraments considerably expands the horizon of priestly service, making it a huge task. It is the magnitude of the task that obliges us to share our active, sacramental service with the laity. Perhaps as the number of priests diminishes, this is God's plan: to engage us in sharing our priestly work with our people, who are called to do such work through their baptism. We must do sincere planning to see how can we involve the faithful in this work, and how and to whom we can entrust certain aspects of sacramental preparation. In the ancient Church preparing people for baptism was the task of catechists, as it is today in the missions

Lay people can visit the sick, console them, bring them holy communion, help them and pray with them. Many young, healthy retired people would be glad to volunteer for whatever ecclesial service that the local church community can entrust to them. Marriage preparation can be better done by Christian couples. Preparation for the Eucharist can profit from the advice and opinions of a parish liturgy committee. The faithful can follow up the progress of the newly baptized and young married couples, and monitor the situation of sick persons in the parish with loving care. This does not mean that the priest gives up his priestly office and service; rather he willingly shares his work with others and co-ordinates the different ministries and ministers. It remains his duty to share and oversee the pastoral work in his parish, and to appear regularly in person, but he does not have to do everything himself.

Let us now examine each phase of this sacramental process. First we will consider the summit of the sacramental process, the celebration itself. Since the primary purpose of every liturgical celebration is to bless God, whenever we celebrate a liturgy, we rejoice that God created us and appreciate all that comes from God's hand. This is the primary purpose of every liturgical celebration. Because of this fundamental attitude of worship, we can receive God's self-communication, life and love. Thus we encounter God through Christ's mysterious presence in the liturgy. Seen this way, no liturgy can be used as a means for reaching a further goal, because liturgy carries in itself its own purpose and meaning, which is nothing other than to experience the presence of salvation and its celebration in Jesus Christ.

Clearly, then, liturgy is not private prayer or recollected meditation. After Vatican II, many people complained that they could not meditate anymore during the Mass, that they were not left in peace to recite the rosary, that they couldn't concentrate on their private devotions because something was always distracting them. A liturgical celebration is neither the time for private prayer nor for concentrated, recollected meditation. Important and necessary as they are, these should take place before the liturgy at home or in the silence of a chapel, since without due preparation it is difficult to create a good liturgy. But when the community gathers to celebrate liturgy, private prayer recedes into the background. It may help if people imagine liturgical celebration as a holy distraction before God. A certain "holy distraction" seems to be part of participating in liturgical action. In the community we, God's children, play before God. This has a deep theological foundation. Distracted in a holy milieu, engaged in "contemplation in action," we are present before God our Father, rejoicing in the life we have received from God. As unselfconscious as children, we express our spiritual experiences in word, song and movement, and open ourselves to an encounter with God that enriches us. Ideally, this would be the tone of our liturgical celebrations: not the rigid attitude (probably left over from a certain Jansenistic influence) of not looking right or left, and modestly closing our eyes after communion so we can be alone with Jesus, and nothing disturb our devotion. Rather, we should rejoice that a little child is running between the pews, that an old man begins to cough, or an altar server makes some mistake, etc. All this is part of the reality of God's people and his holy play! We should accept calmly and naturally that these things happen in God's family. Celebration is thus solemn, dignified and extraordinary—and yet intimate, a total experience, not just an intellectual one, for the sacred symbols work on all the senses. Liturgy therefore has no other purpose but our communion with God, Christ and one another in the framework of the Church. This is the goal of our life both now and in heaven.

The first phase of the liturgical process is preparation. Preparation happens en route to the summit. During this period we collect the spiritual experiences and build up in our prayer and spiritual life the habitual attitudes such as faith, hope, love, dedication, humility that we bring to liturgy and express in word, deed and song. What are these spiritual experiences? They include prayer and immersion in the mysteries of our faith through study or spiritual reading; simple, spontaneous prayers that spring from our hearts in joy, or sorrow, examinations of conscience, sincere contrition, experiences of our sinfulness and God's forgiving love. Other experiences also belong here: encounters with God or Christ in nature—when we are touched by God's immense greatness in contemplating the vast expanse of oceans or the huge Rocky Mountains; encounters with people, with good and holy men and women, with everyday saints; daily self denials, when we die a little bit to ourselves to live for others, or practice charity, or spend some time in prayer before the tabernacle. We gather up these spiritual experiences in preparation for whichever sacramental celebration comes next.

More immediate preparation consists in studying and meditating on the texts of the sacramental liturgy. This is the place for private meditative prayer. The scripture and liturgical texts express beautifully the spirituality that constitutes the inner content of the liturgy. It is simply not acceptable to begin to search for the appropriate text in the Missal or Ritual once the liturgy has begun. Presiders should read and meditate on these texts beforehand so they understand their theological and spiritual significance. The liturgical books offer us enough material for meditation to last a lifetime! The words we say should flow from our own inner dispositions lest our liturgy may become an exercise in pure formality that was condemned not only by the prophets, but also by Our Lord. This is the first phase of the sacramental process.

The third phase is nothing other than the continuation of the liturgy, its outcome in our everyday life—the "liturgy of life," as Rahner, among others, put it. It is an important pastoral task to put liturgical experience into practice in everyday life. One way to do this is by regular, periodical renewal of sacramental moments, such as the renewal of baptismal promises at the Easter Vigil, of ordination promises on the anniversary of ordination or at the Chrism Mass, or marriage vows on wedding anniversaries. Thus we can realize that sacramental grace continues to be effective throughout our lives. Theologically it is certain that the effect of sacramental grace extends not only to the celebrative moments of the sacrament, but also to both the preparatory phase and its implementation in the course of life. In ancient Christian times this continuous deepening in the mysteries was called "*mystagogia*." Our whole Christian life, our whole priestly or married life, is a gradual penetration into the mystery of baptism, holy orders, or marriage. From this viewpoint the liturgical texts could be truly the school of our prayer.

Thanksgiving after the sacramental liturgy also belongs to this third phase. We are used to doing this after our eucharistic celebrations in the thanksgiving after Mass. It is an opportunity to express our gratitude for all those graces and gifts that we received in the sacraments and in the liturgy. We can and should base our whole Christian moral life on our sacramental life. This means that every one of our moral actions arises out of the sacraments and corresponds to their requirements. We could examine our faults and sins in this light: do we live up to our baptismal or marriage vows?

The missionary work of the Church is also rooted in the liturgy. At the end of Mass we hear the dismissal: "Go, in the peace of Christ." This is the time of sending, of mission. One of the ancient Christian texts expresses this attitude in this way: "Go, hurry now, everyone should strive to do good deeds, that is, to live according to what you celebrated in the Eucharist" (*Festinet nunc unusquisque opera bona facere!*). The whole mission of the Church, including its social services, the diakonia, what we do for the sake of the world, originates in this fountain. But this is especially applicable to the building up of the Christian community, the Church, since the liturgy produces the Church. Every liturgical action ought to strengthen our determination to be a better, more active member of the Mystical Body of Christ, the Church, especially of that concrete, local church to which we belong.

Part II

LITURGIES OF THE SACRAMENTS

Chapter 10

THE LITURGY OF CHRISTIAN INITIATION

People are not born Christian; they become Christian. This chapter will explore the process of becoming a Christian. According to the tradition of the Church, Christian initiation happens through three sacraments: baptism, confirmation, and Eucharist. People become fully Christian and full members of the Church only through these three sacraments. Closely connected, the three taken together indicate that Christian initiation is not a momentary event, but a process of maturing in the faith, characterized by the liturgies of these three sacraments.

The sacraments of Christian initiation raise some theological problems. One problem arises from the custom of infant baptism. In the Western Catholic Church confirmation follows some ten to fifteen years later, but in between children already receive the sacrament of forgiveness and holy communion. According to some theologians, this does not correspond to the ancient order of sacraments, baptism–confirmation followed by Eucharist and the other sacraments.

The other problem is that baptism, like any sacrament, presupposes faith. Many consider baptism the beginning of our faith life: the seed of faith sown by God in the human heart begins to grow slowly and may develop into a large tree. Others, for example, the Anabaptists, maintain that baptism crowns our growth in faith, therefore it should happen only when the individual is sufficiently mature in their faith. After World War II, Karl Barth also attacked the general practice of infant baptism from the Protestant side, suggesting that the baptism of children should be postponed until they are able to ask for this sacrament of faith. At the present time none of the Christian churches that performs infant baptism is willing to give up or abandon the custom.

Another important theological question is: what is the effect of baptism? Its primary effect is to incorporate the individual into the Church, making them members of the Church through the sacramental character. Whether they receive the grace of the sacrament or not, they are marked forever with this sacramental character, which means that they cannot and must not, be re-baptized. Sacramental character makes them members of Christ's Mystical Body and participants in Christ's priesthood. The texts of the baptismal ritual express well this communal, ecclesial character of baptism with its far-reaching pastoral consequences.

Baptism confers sanctifying grace. This grace actually is nothing other than the coming of the Holy Spirit in our heart and the result of his indwelling. This may become clearer if we point out our relationship with each of the three divine persons of the Holy Trinity. Through sanctifying grace we become children of the Father to whom we owe loving obedience and to whom we are to surrender ourselves. Practically, this means that we must renounce selfishness and self-centredness to seek, accept and follow God's will rather than our own.

Sanctifying grace also builds us into the Body of Christ or, as St. Paul would say, inserts us into Christ. Consequently we commit ourselves in baptism to live the life of Christ: "The life I now live is not my life, but the life which Christ lives in me" says St. Paul (Gal. 2:20). This means that we should be configured to the life of Christ; the image of Christ should be visible in us; we should act and behave as he would; we should listen to his heartbeat. St. Paul uses quite specific words to describe our mystical symbiosis with Christ: we live with Christ, die with Christ, are risen with Christ, we reign with Christ, etc. Most significantly, we are joined to his paschal mystery, so that we live it out every day of our lives, especially in the hour of death. Christians commit themselves to all this when they receive the sacrament. Sanctifying grace also manifests the presence of the Holy Spirit in our heart. We relate to the Holy Spirit by recognizing his presence in us; we let him direct our lives, and listen to his inspiration; we become spiritual persons who develop a prayerful inner life. At the same time the Holy Spirit also impels us to witness to this divine gift and life in the outside world.

Every sacrament means a certain commitment. God makes such a commitment to us, and we should not hesitate to promise sincerely that we are going to live as children of the Father, members of Christ's body, temples of the Holy Spirit, and organic parts of the Church. This commitment takes place in the baptismal liturgy and remains in effect for our whole life. We can say that our Christian life is simply the daily living out and practice of the sacrament of baptism.

Through baptism we become members of the Church. The Church of Christ, to which all Christians belong regardless of the denomination in which they have been baptized, grows through this sacrament. Still, every baptized person is baptized into a local church, a parish community. The universal Church is the communion (*koinonia*) of the local churches. There is no such a thing as a freelance Christian who doesn't want to belong to any church or parish. This is the ecclesial character of our baptism. Baptism connects us with a real, specific community. This means that the local community has to take the reception of new members very seriously. Every parish has a missionary obligation to acquire new members, receive them with love, and care for them as they progress through the stages of becoming Christian. Only in this way can they become organic parts of the local church and active members of the community.

The renewed baptismal ritual rightly emphasizes the community's role. This is even clearer in the Rite of Christian Initiation of Adults, which restores the initiatory process of the ancient Church. This restoration indicates that adult baptism is the prototype, the primary example, of baptism, even if most of those the Church baptizes today are infants. The RCIA imposes on us the obligation to pay more attention to the whole process of initiation, especially to the catechumenate, which helps candidates grow in faith until they arrive at the celebration of baptism.

If adult baptism is the prototype, then it also ought to influence our view of infant baptism, although other viewpoints must also be taken into account.

The process of adult initiation consists of several parts. The first is the period of evangelization and precatechumenate, when someone who begins to be interested in the Christian religion, sympathizes with it, listens to the word of God, reads about it and discusses it with other Christians. Gradually under the influence of divine grace they may come to the point of wanting to believe. At this point the catechumenate begins; in the ancient Church it lasted two or three years. During this period the Christian community helps and supports the catechumens as they get to know Christian life, not only intellectually—through religious instruction, but practically. They learn how Christians should behave in different situations of daily life; in other words, how to live an active Christian life. The catechumenate is a kind of novitiate during which the community assumes responsibility for introducing the catechumens into the Christian lifestyle.

The last period of the catechumenate, the period of illumination, or enlightenment, normally coincides with Lent. During Lent the catechumens begin to be more and more aware of what they are undertaking through scripture readings, and especially through the texts of the "scrutinies"; the elect are presented with the specifically Christian texts, the Apostles' Creed and the Lord's Prayer, in preparation for the celebration of the sacrament of baptism, which normally takes place at the Easter Vigil. On that holy night, in the midst of the Christian community, the elect are baptized and confirmed, and participate for the first time in the sacred action of the Eucharist. All three sacraments are celebrated together at this occasion.

The final period of adult initiation is called "*mystagogia.*" According to ancient Christian practice it took place during Easter week. In this week the newly baptized participated every day in the Eucharist and listened to the mystagogical catecheses of the bishop. These provided an insight into the mysteries. It is interesting to note that during the catechumenate, there was no instruction about the sacraments. The catechumens were introduced into the Christian tradition; they heard the biblical stories, the mysterious work of God in the Old and New Testament, and in history; they became familiar with the mysteries of the life of Christ; in other words, they were introduced into the traditional lore of the Christian family so that their mentality, their world view, might become truly Christian. They were also taught how to behave as Christians, how to discern the ways of light and darkness, what behaviours were right and wrong.

They participated in the liturgy of the word, in the prayer and charitable activities of the community, but they were not told about the sacraments. They received the sacraments Easter night without knowing much about their essence and process. Because the ancient Christian Church treated the sacraments as ecclesial secrets which they kept from the uninitiated, the catechumens received their first instruction about them in the period of mystagogy only after they had already celebrated them. Why? Because the ancient Church held that no one can perceive the sacred mysteries without having experienced them before. Only after celebrating baptism, confirmation and Eucharist, only after participating in these wonderful events, can these new Christians realize the sacred mysteries in which they have just participated.

The Church thus considers adult initiation as the prototype of Christian initiation. In our regions this may not occur very often, (except in mission territories), but since in the future we will have more such cases, it would be worthwhile to pay more attention to it by setting up the catechumenate, or RCIA programs. The essence of this program is that the Christian community assumes the responsibility of introducing the candidates into Christian life, because the candidate will be baptized into the faith of these faithful Christians.

From the process of adult initiation we can also learn and apply certain essential points to the more common practice of infant baptism, which should also be part of a process. In the ancient church it was customary for Christian parents to bring their children for baptism so their children could become members of the Church and receive God's regenerating grace. Faith is also required for infant baptism, but it is the faith of the parents and the Christian community on which infant baptism is based. Parents, godparents and the community assume the task of providing an environment in which the seed of faith sown in the heart of the child can develop and unfold into personal faith. For this reason the Church requires that parents be instructed before baptism so that they realize their responsibility in asking that their child be baptized.

The Church believes that in baptism sanctifying grace takes away original sin and all personal sins (which in the case of infants are not yet present). Baptism therefore cleanses us from all sins. This negative effect of baptism is well expressed by washing with water. But baptism also has a positive effect, symbolized by the baptismal water, that living water that comes from the side of Christ and brings us new life. We can speak therefore, of a negative and a positive effect of baptism.

In the history of the Church, the sacrament of initiation was divided into two parts for different reasons: the sacrament of baptism and the sacrament of confirmation. Theologically we say that the one sacrament of initiation happens in two phases. One phase, by the washing with water, expresses more clearly the negative effect that is liberation from the dirt of sin; the other, through the imposition of hands and the sealing with the chrism, indicates more clearly the positive effect that is the coming of the Holy Spirit and new life. Both sacraments signify the effect but neither does so exclusively, because the Holy Spirit has already come into our hearts at baptism. Baptism directs our attention more clearly to the fact that the baptized are freed from their sins and taken out of the realm of darkness into the kingdom of light; in confirmation the new life and presence of the Holy Spirit in the heart of the baptized is expressed more solemnly.

There are historical reasons for the chronological separation of these two sacraments. In the first centuries, when the bishop baptized everyone, he administered both sacraments at the same time. Later, because of the great number of baptisands, priests in the Western Church normally baptized, but they did not confirm because the Church desired that during the process of becoming a Christian the neophytes meet the bishop, who represents the Christian community, in person. So the Western Church delayed confirmation until the bishop came to complete and crown the process of initiation.

The Rite of Christian Initiation of Children consists of four parts. Under ideal circumstances each of the four parts takes place at different locations in the Church.

(1) The reception of the children or infants normally takes place at the door of the church, where the presider greets parents, godparents, and other family members quite informally, congratulating them on the birth of their child, and, in the name of the church, thanking them for bringing the child for baptism. In this initial dialogue

The Liturgy of Christian Initiation

we ask the name of their child, and remind the parents and godparents of their responsibility for the Christian upbringing of their child. The important liturgical sign at this point is signing the child's forehead with the sign of the cross, whereby we claim and mark him for Jesus Christ. Signing with the sign of the cross *(consignatio)* is an ancient Christian custom, which has biblical roots, since it is the sign that, according to the Apocalypse, remains in heaven. The sign of our baptism is written on our forehead. This signing should take place solemnly. Invite parents, godparents and other family members to sign the child with the sign of the cross, too.

(2) After this brief introduction we move in procession to the body of the church, where the second part of the ritual is celebrated. The procession is already a liturgical sign, since when we enter the church, the child enters the Church of God, the Christian community symbolized by the church building. This second part takes place around the ambo. There we listen as the word of God is proclaimed. We respond with a psalm, spoken or sung, and the prayer of the faithful. The homily should bring the mysterious presence of Christ closer to us, since it is Christ who "administers" the sacrament. Here we also perform the so-called "minor exorcism" through anointing with the oil of catechumens (OS or OC) and the imposition of hands. Exorcism in this case is nothing other than the effective supplication of the Church for this baptisand, asking God to deliver this child from darkness and evil, and to give them strength to live the Christian life, for through baptism the child is transferred from the power of darkness to the kingdom of light: "Almighty God, you sent your only Son to rescue us from the slavery of sin, and to give us the freedom only your sons and daughters enjoy. We pray now for this child who will have to face the world with its temptations, and fight the devil in all his cunning. Your Son died and rose again to save us. By his victory over sin and death, cleanse this child from the stain of original sin. Strengthen him/her with the grace of Christ, and watch over him/her at every step in life's journey." (*Rite of Baptism of Children,* 170B).

Since the sign of exorcism is normally the imposition of hands, it would be advisable to underline this gesture after the prayer by silently laying hands on the child for a few seconds. Only then would the anointing, which is also a symbol of the Holy Spirit's power, take place.

To enhance the solemnity of the occasion, sing during the procession from one place to another. In some parishes, where baptism is celebrated once a month on Sunday afternoon, the whole parish community is invited to participate. On such an occasion the baptisands, their families, the altar-servers and the priest move in procession.

This raises the question of the community's role in the celebration, and should make each community examine its conscience: can we accept new members if we do not have a real, living Christian community? We should first pay attention to creating a real Christian community out of those who are already members of the Church; then we can accept new ones, otherwise into what do we accept them? We cannot and should not simply use the excuse that because baptism works *"ex opere operato,"* once the baptismal water is poured, the newly baptized quasi-automatically becomes a Christian. Baptism becomes effective within a concrete parish community, because this is how the seed of faith, God's grace in the heart of the child, develops and unfolds. For this reason the revised rite indicates that we should not baptize children whose parents do not want to, or cannot assure, their Christian education. Although the Church urges that children be baptized shortly after their birth, if the parents or larger family environment cannot assure the growth of the child's faith, it is better to postpone the baptism. We should, however, maintain contact with that family and, with pastoral prudence, help them to create a Christian milieu in their homes, where the growth of the child's faith is guaranteed.

(3) The third part of the rite of baptism of children happens at the baptismal font. In some churches, this occupies a privileged spot; in some places it has running water. It would be ideal if we had more fonts in which we could baptize by immersion. The baptismal font indicates our rebirth from above. Therefore we should strive to make it attractive as a lasting reminder of the solemn moment of baptism and its mystery. Beside the fountain should stand the paschal candle, the symbol of the risen Christ. During the preparation and celebration of baptism we should try to awaken in the whole community the magnificence of the Christian vocation and the fundamental importance of baptism. We remember this at least once a year at the Easter Vigil when we renew our baptismal vows after our Lenten preparation

The Liturgy of Christian Initiation

for this moment. And, on the anniversary of our baptism, or whenever we take part in a baptism, we can re-experience our own baptism, and all that happened to us when we were touched by the life-giving water and the Spirit.

At the baptismal font the water is blessed first, except during the Easter season when we simply say a thanksgiving prayer over the water already blessed at the Easter Vigil. When the priest blesses the water, he touches it with his hand, (another *epiklesis* with imposition of hands): "We ask you, Father, with your Son to send the Holy Spirit upon the water of this font." This is a pentecost moment: the Holy Spirit descends upon the water, so that through the water he may confer sanctifying grace to the baptized person. The blessing of the baptismal water is followed by the renunciation of Satan and the profession of faith. These are based on the rite of the covenant in the Old Testament, with which Moses and his successors renewed their covenant with the Lord. In baptism this covenant is actualized.

The covenant rite includes a negative and a positive moment. On the one hand, we remember and reject Satan; on the other, we promise, surrender, commit ourselves through the profession of faith to the Father, Son and Holy Spirit. The ancient Christian Church also expressed this in movement: first the baptized turned toward the West, the symbol of darkness, and renounced Satan and his pomps, and even spit upon him as a sign of the complete rejection of evil. From the West they turned to the East, the symbol of light *(Ex Oriente lux)*. The turning around (*conversio, metanoia*) means that someone here now turns from the way of darkness to the light, Christ himself. Actually, this covenant rite was, in the ancient Church, the sacramental formula of baptism. The present short formula, "I baptize you in the name of the Father, and of the Son, and of the Holy Spirit," became customary in the West only in the sixth and seventh centuries. Previously they had baptized by a threefold immersion, and they posed a question at each immersion: "Do you believe in the Father ... in the Son ... in the Holy Spirit ..." to which the baptized answered: I believe. When the short formula was introduced, the threefold commitment and profession of faith had been placed where we find it today, before the actual baptism.

Here, then, is the solemn moment when the baptisand is joined to the body of Christ. It should be marked with some kind of acclamation, if possible.

Among the rites that follow baptism, the first is the anointing with chrism, the scented oil that is also the symbol of the Holy Spirit who anointed Christ as Messiah. Through this anointing the baptized person becomes "Christic," anointed to that messianic vocation that manifests itself in priestly, prophetic, royal activity. Then the child is then clothed with a white robe that indicates Christian dignity, since the baptized person is now clothed in Christ. The lighted candle speaks of the light of faith and grace, signifying that the baptized person ought to walk through life as a child of light. It is the task of the mother to hold the child in her arms during the whole ritual.

The godmother should prepare the white vestment and dress the child in it. The child's father holds the lighted candle for the child, and the candle should be lit from the paschal candle. This concludes the ritual at the font, and now we move again in procession to the altar.

(4) The fourth part of the ritual takes place at the main altar, indicating that baptism leads to the celebration of the Eucharist. At the altar we pray the Lord's Prayer, our family prayer, together. Once again the priest reminds the parents that baptism is but the beginning of the process of becoming a Christian. They will have to lead the child first to the sacrament of confirmation, and then to the Eucharist. Finally the priest gives a threefold blessing; first, to the mother, then to the father and finally, to all those present, and then dismisses them.

Although the traditional order of the sacraments of Initiation is baptism–confirmation– Eucharist, the Church in many countries has allowed children to receive holy communion around the age of 7, even though they are not yet confirmed. There is no contradiction in this. After some preparation, when children can distinguish between ordinary bread and the Eucharist (for example, "the Lord Jesus comes into my heart in the host"), then they can participate in this heavenly food, which was already in the first centuries called the "daily bread." But children can only actively participate in the celebration of the eucharistic mystery if they can to perceive with their minds what it means to be a Christian, what it means to unite themselves with the sacrifice of Christ and offer themselves to the Father in loving surrender. When children get to this point during their catechetical formation, (and it is rather difficult to state, generally, at what age it happens), then the time is ripe for confirmation and for active participation in the eucharistic event.

The renewed ritual of baptism emphasizes the role of the local people, the Christian community, in receiving new members. The Christian community ought to also think of those semi-Christians who were baptized in infancy, but who never practised their faith for some reason and now want to join the life of the community. For them we might organize adult catechesis in the style of the catechumenate, or even a lecture series that both they and the people who sincerely live a Christian life can attend. Such a process would not only offer intellectual formation, but would gradually enable them to join the prayer, the liturgical, social, apostolic life of the community. For those baptized in infancy such a "catechumenate" exists: catechesis that follows baptism and develops and nurtures in them the seed of faith, introducing them into a Christian life not only through religion classes, but also through liturgical and social activities, prayer and the practice of Christian charity.

In our days there is much discussion about the proper age for Confirmation. The question cannot be decided purely on historical or theoretical grounds. In each country, pastoral consideration must enter into deciding what is the optimal and most practical age for the completion of the initiation process with confirmation. One thing is certain, whether one is baptized and confirmed in infancy, or baptized in infancy and confirmed later, there must be a period of catechesis or introduction into Christian life, provided by the family, by religious instruction in the school, and by the Christian community at large. Sooner or later each baptized person must come to a conscious recognition of their Christian identity, and accept their baptismal commitment personally, consciously and freely, thus ratifying the profession of faith that was made at the time of their baptism. In our Western society this may coincide with the time young people begin to think of the meaning of life and of choosing some direction in life. This may occur around the age of fourteen or fifteen or later, depending on circumstances. It is a time of a kind of "fundamental option" for which each person has to be prepared both intellectually and practically.

One way to prepare is to consider Christian life as a family. Through baptism people are accepted into God's family, the Church, and have to grow in it as an infant, as a child, as a young man or woman. Like children in a family, they learn through their family story over the years: the story of God's fatherly love and care in the Old Testament, and then especially in the New, the story of Jesus from the Gospels. They have to become familiar with their family history after the biblical times, the history of the Church throughout the centuries, the history of the Church in their own nation, and the story of the saints. Here they belong: "God is my Father, Jesus is my brother, Mary is my mother, the Christians around the world are my brothers and sisters." They know them or at least know *about* them. They also learn the different symbols of their family, because symbols join us together more effectively than words. They become familiar with the liturgical symbols in the church: the altar, the baptismal font, the icons, the statues, etc. They know the special feast days of their family: Christmas, Easter, feasts of Christ, Mary, and the saints. They feel at home every Sunday when they go to Mass. They have learned and can recite their family's prayers: the Lord's Prayer, the Hail Mary, the Creed, etc. They know and often read the Bible, which contains much of their family's tradition. They have learned how to behave as members of this Christian family. As children, they have learned from adults how to be honest, truthful, and reliable; how to be unselfish, generous and charitable; how to be pure and faithful. They know what to do when they fail in their moral behaviour, how to seek forgiveness from God and from others, how to forgive others when they have offended us. They are active members of their local parish community and/or its organizations: youth-club, altar-servers, etc. They know how to be joyful and optimistic about their future, how to hope for better times to come, how to long for heaven.

When they are preparing for confirmation, they consider seriously the baptismal vows that were made when they were baptized and which they will renew at the rite of confirmation as their ratification of what happened earlier. They commit themselves to the Holy Trinity, to each of the three divine persons.

The Liturgy of Christian Initiation

"I believe in the Father, who is the Almighty Creator and therefore can do whatever he wants, who at the same time is also my loving Father who always wants the best for me. I believe in and commit myself to Jesus Christ who loved me so much that he died for me that I may live. I want to live his life, to be as unselfish as he was, living for others rather than for myself, willing to make sacrifices, willing to die with him so that I may rise with him and live with him forever. I believe in the Holy Spirit who dwells in me, and to whom I listen. He teaches me how to pray, how to become a spiritual person, how to interiorize whatever I learned from Jesus. He also impels me to witness to the many gifts I have received, and especially to the paschal mystery, the joy that awaits us. I commit myself to be an active, member of the Church, who builds up the local community to which I belong, which is my family. Through my life I want to contribute to this holy, one, catholic and apostolic Church. In this Church, I find my shelter, my home, my consolation despite the many faults of its human face. And I put my hope in this Church where God has chosen to dwell."*

With this kind of preparation they can look forward with great joy and expectation to the celebration when the bishop lays his hand upon them and signs them with the holy chrism in the form of the cross (*consignatio*), marking them forever as members of Christ, a mark which they will also carry proudly in heaven.

The third sacrament of the initiation process is the Eucharist. This is not just the reception of holy communion that accompanies our progress on the way to maturation as our daily food, but Eucharist as a full, active, conscious celebration and participation in the eucharistic mystery with its paschal transformation. We will deal with this eucharistic liturgy in the following chapter. The regular, weekly or even daily celebration of the Eucharist always renews our baptismal commitment, and actualizes our immersion in the paschal mystery.

---

* *Rite of Baptism for Children.* Ottawa: Canadian Conference of Catholic Bishops, 1989, no. 58, p.29.

Chapter 11

THE LITURGY OF THE EUCHARIST

Vatican II reminded us again of what every Catholic Christian knew anyhow: the Eucharist is the source and summit of our whole Christian life. The liturgical celebration of the Eucharist has undergone quite a development through the centuries. In the first millennium it was much more evident how the three dimensions of the eucharistic mystery—the real presence of Christ, the sacrificial action of the Holy Mass and the holy communion—belong together. Over time, for different historical and theological reasons, this strict unity between the three dimensions loosened considerably, and so theology began to treat them separately; our liturgical practice has followed this divergence in the last few centuries. Holy communion was rarely received during Mass, because this occurred either before Mass or after. From the 13th century on, the various eucharistic devotions placed great emphasis on the adoration of the Real Presence of Christ. While all three dimensions of the eucharistic mystery are important, and it is understandable that in every age one or the other receives more attention, this division of the one mystery lessened the unified view of the Eucharist, and sometimes even led to mistaken practices. The twentieth-century liturgical movement tried to correct this somewhat until Vatican II once again restored the unity of the eucharistic mystery.

My intention here is not to analyze the whole theology of the Eucharist, but rather to discuss its liturgical celebration, especially the central part of the eucharistic mystery, the eucharistic prayer. In the West, this is called the *Canon,* in the East it is known as the

Anaphora: recently, we have begun to use the ancient expression "eucharistic prayer" *(Prex Eucharistica).* The eucharistic prayer does not exhaust the whole celebration of the Mass, which also includes the liturgy of the word, the preparation of the gifts, communion rite, and the concluding section, which are all important and integral parts of the Mass. The central part, however, is still the Canon, which begins with the priest's invitation: "Lift up your hearts!" *(Sursum corda)* and concludes with the doxology and the solemn Amen. I will now address this prayer in the light of more recent theological insights.

This deeper insight into the mystery is important for us because the eucharistic prayer is like our daily bread; we recite it every day, but we hardly realize how full of the deepest theological content and spiritual food it is. From a theological viewpoint this prayer is one of the most important sources of our theologizing, superseded in importance only by Holy Scripture itself. Just as Scripture is "the book of the Church," so the eucharistic prayer is "the prayer of the Church," which the Church produces and adopts as her own expression of faith. In this prayer we find the eucharistic mystery, which in ancient Christian times was shrouded in secrecy; it was not even written down for fear that it fall into the hands of enemies of the Church *(disciplina arcani).*

Today liturgical theology looks on this prayer as the one, unified, unique consecratory prayer of the Eucharist. To some ears this may sound a bit unusual because the essentialist method of scholastic theology saw the essential consecratory formula in the words of the Lord *(verba Dominica)* alone: "This is my Body ..., This is my Blood ...." Today, recalling the first thousand years' practice of the Church, we recognize that the whole eucharistic prayer is consecratory. There are certain peak moments in the prayer, the *epiklesis* and the pronunciation of the words of the Lord, but these peak moments cannot be isolated from the context of the whole prayer. It is therefore a unified, priestly prayer, pronounced by the head, the authorized and ordained leader, the priest, who speaks in the name of Christ and "in the person of Christ," the Head of the Church *(in persona Christi capitis).*

This prayer originates in Scripture because our Eucharist arises from the Last Supper. The three synoptic gospels and 1 Corinthians

The Liturgy of the Eucharist

describe what happened in the room of the Last Supper; but unfortunately this description is a rather terse presentation of the event. The historical account of the Last Supper then entered our eucharistic prayer from the scriptures. What do these accounts tell us? When the Lord Jesus came together with his disciples to celebrate and eat the traditional paschal meal (*seder pesach*), he took the bread, said the blessing, broke the bread and distributed it to them with these words: "Take it and eat it, this is my body." He did the same with the cup, took it into his hands, said the blessing, and gave it to his disciples to drink with these words: "This is the cup of my blood." This is not the place to analyze these essential, fundamental, creative words of the Lord, theologically important though they are. We presuppose all that the Church teaches in this respect. However, the connection of the texts deserves attention. Scripture describes the Lord's action in four parts, out of which our eucharistic action has developed. First, during the preparation of the gifts (*offertorium*), we take the bread and wine. Rightly speaking, this is not an offering, but simply the preparation of the sacrificial gifts. The second action follows: pronouncing the blessing over the bread and wine. The third action, the breaking of bread, is still part of the Mass. Finally comes the fourth action, sharing the consecrated bread and drinking from the cup in holy communion.

Our primary interest is the blessing that the Lord Jesus said at the Last Supper. It would be a misinterpretation of the text to assume that the Lord took the bread and the cup, and blessed them with some kind of formula, such as the priest would use to bless certain foods on Easter Sunday. The right translation is that the Lord said a "blessing prayer" (*berakah*). By the fifth century some people who were specially interested in the text of the blessing that the Lord said over the bread and wine had gently rebuked the evangelists for their terse account of the Last Supper. Studying this blessing has led most liturgical scholars today to maintain that the origin of this blessing prayer can be sought in the text and structure of the Jewish Passover meal, which is still used among the Jews at the celebration of Passover. It is well known that at the end of each of the four parts of the Jewish seder, the participants drink from the cup. The text therefore speaks of four cups. The first part of the ritual offers an introduction and blessing over the different symbolic foods. The second part consists of teaching, in which the story of the exodus from Egypt is recited in question and answer form. The third part is the actual supper at which the paschal lamb is eaten. But before participants begin to eat, they say a short blessing over the unleavened bread (*matzot*). After they finish the lamb, they drink the third cup. At this point, a longer prayer of blessing, which is today, even as it was at the time of Jesus, the grace after meals (*birkat-ha-mazon*) is pronounced. The fourth part of the paschal meal, thanksgivings and singing of psalms which the biblical account mentions, follows.

If we imagine the Last Supper in this setting, we can understand that when the Lord "said the blessing," the scriptures refer to the blessing over the bread, in particular, the blessing over the third cup. St. Paul calls this third cup "the cup of blessing" *(poterion tes eulogias),* because this blessing was so important and central that it gave the title to the cup connected with it. Recent liturgical investigations have discovered that the most ancient extant eucharistic prayer, the Anaphora of Addai and Mari of the East Syrian Liturgy, which most probably originates from the second or third century, corresponds structurally, content-wise and even in its key words, to the Jewish text of the *birkat-ha-mazon* and its structure. Later eucharistic prayers manifest the same structure and content.

All that I have said in previous chapters about the *berakah* is important for understanding the content of the eucharistic prayer properly. As the fundamental act of worship and basic attitude of the Jewish and Christian religions, it provides us with the context in which we can read these accounts. When the Lord Jesus at the Last Supper wanted to make present the sacrifice of his life that he would offer the next day on the cross, he said a blessing, a *berakah* in the context of the paschal meal. He praised and blessed God, thus perfectly expressing what every human being ought to do by the sheer fact of being a creature. Adam was supposed to have done this, but he failed. Now the second Adam blesses God with his whole life by completely accepting the creaturely existence of his human nature and his utter dependence on God.

The literary form of the eucharistic prayer is therefore blessing and praise, *berakah*. The Greek translation uses two words to express the rich content of the Hebrew *berakah*: *eulogia* and *eucharistia*.

The meaning of two words is almost the same, yet a slight difference distinguishes them. *Eulogia* normally means to say good about or praise someone. We bless and praise God, because he is above all, the Creator God, who can do whatever he wants. Joyfully we acknowledge his goodness, greatness, holiness: this is pure, unselfish blessing and praising of God. The other word, *eucharistia,* is somewhat different because it means thanksgiving, returning thanks for the gifts and great benefits *(magnalia Dei)* that we have received during our salvation history. Pure praise acknowledges that we are creatures and God, the Creator God and Lord above everything: the One who created every being and life itself. Because life is good and beautiful, we bless and praise God. In thanksgiving, on the other hand, God appears not only as Creator God, but as God of the Covenant, the covenant-partner who walks with us on the way of our salvation history. Because God showers us with benefits, we turn to him with gratitude; we give God thanks and praise.

We bless and praise God in words and deeds. We praise God with words when we sing hymns, chant psalms and shout Alleluias; we praise God with deeds when we bring symbolic gifts in return for his goodness to us. This latter happens in the form of small everyday sacrifices, or the complete surrender of our lives at death. This action of blessing and praising God is the main content of every celebration. The first goal of every liturgical celebration is to express this inner attitude of the human person.

Berakah has still another translation in Greek: *exomologesis,* which means acknowledgement or confession. Whenever the New Testament quotes the prayer of the Lord Jesus, this word always appears at the beginning. For example: "I acknowledge you and I praise you, Father, Lord of heaven and earth, for hiding these things from the learned and wise … " (Mt.11:25). When Jesus prays before raising Lazarus from death, he uses this same word (Jn.11:41). The Latin translation of *exomologesis* is *confessio*, indicating that the word "confession" comes from *berakah*. Whenever we make a confession, we confess, that is, acknowledge, God as the true reality, and our utter dependence on him. This applies even to the confession of sins in the sacrament of reconciliation: here too, we first confess God's greatness and holiness and, especially, God's kindness and mercy.

The psalms are full of different synonyms of *berakah*. It is worthwhile to scan them for words that freely praise God and bless him, that unselfconsciously and unselfishly rejoice and shout: mountains and valleys, sun and moon, flowers and trees, wind, snow and ice, everything should praise the Lord! The psalter is full of this kind of praise.

The psalms often turn from pure praise of God to thanksgiving, speaking of the great deeds of God *(magnalia Dei):* how much we have received from God, and how grateful we are for all these gifts—therefore we bless him! Our doxologies also express this *berakah*. That is why we say the doxology after every psalm and on other occasions: so that this attitude may penetrate our whole being and our whole life continuously praise God.

If we examine the content of the *berakah*, we can learn how Jesus prayed and what he said when he instituted the Eucharist. The original *birkat-ha-mazon* is a rather lengthy prayer consisting of three parts or pericopes. The first pericope begins with the words: "Blessed are you, LORD, our God, King of the whole universe ... " *"Baruk atta, Yahweh Elohenu, melek ha-olam."* "Blessed are You, because you feed the whole world with your goodness. You created this universe and you give bread in your mercy to all living beings, you sustain us in existence by giving us food. You feed all creatures that you have created. And for this we bless you and praise you." This first pericope is pure praise of the Creator God. Its theological content is this: the LORD is the Creator who created everything, who produced life itself, who sustains this life by giving us food at all times. Food always directs our attention to the fact that God sustains the world in being. So this first pericope is called *oratio theologica*, i.e. theological prayer, prayer about God.

The second pericope of the *birkat-ha-mazon* focuses on thanksgiving. It begins: "We give you thanks, LORD, our God ... " *"Node leka."* "We give you thanks because you promised the Promised Land to our fathers, led them out of Egypt, brought them into Canaan; you entered into a covenant with them, you gave them the Law to direct their lives. You give us life, grace, mercy, and you care for us day by day. For all these we thank you and we praise you."

The Liturgy of the Eucharist

In this second part we turn to the God of the Covenant, who walks with the people of Israel during their history, performing his magnificent deeds that enable us to experience how much God loves us. We are grateful for these and praise him. Here we deal not so much with unselfish, pure praise, but rather with gratitude for the gifts received. This too belongs to the concept of *berakah*.

The third pericope begins: "Be kind and have mercy on us, LORD, our God ..." *(Rahem)*. "Especially be gracious to your people, to your city Jerusalem, and the house of David, your anointed one. Our Father and our God, lead us as a Good Shepherd and feed us. Come among us, be with us on our way, remember how much you did for our fathers and for us in the past, and do it also in the future. Especially build up Jerusalem, your holy city. For all these once again we bless you and praise you." As we can see, this third pericope consists of petitions: we ask God to be with us in the future, just as he was our companion in the past. We ask God to come among us, that through his presence his holy city may be built up.

So the *birkat-ha-mazon* consists of three parts: pure praise of God, thanksgiving and petition for the Lord's presence now and in the future, and petition for continuing presence, that he may gather his people into one and build up Jerusalem. This is most probably the prayer that the Lord used at the Last Supper when he instituted the Eucharist and gave himself to us under the species of bread and wine. This structure and essential content are present in all the ancient eucharistic prayers. Of course, the Jewish prayer underwent some stylistic changes on the lips of the Lord Jesus: he called God his "Father," not "LORD," and when he spoke about building up Jerusalem, he spoke about the New Jerusalem that is his Church. The Christian community needed to add to the enumeration of God's magnificent deeds, since beyond the events of the Old Testament, God's greatest benefit was Jesus Christ and his redemptive life work.

We can find the structure and content of the *birkat-ha-mazon* in our current eucharistic prayers. Eucharistic Prayer I (the Roman Canon), which has such great authority and tradition in the Western Church, cannot be used as an example because its structure has been disturbed. The best example is Eucharistic Prayer IV, which we will now examine.

The first part of Eucharistic Prayer IV corresponds to the first pericope of the *birkat-ha-mazon*, pure praise of the Creator God. Look at the text: "It is right that we should give you thanks and glory; you alone are God, Holy Father, living and true ... " Mark the words: thanks and glory—that is, *berakah*. We call God "Holy Father": "holy" means the sovereign, transcendent God, who at the same time is also our Father. "You alone are God" – *unus es Deus*. This is evidently the Jewish and Christian profession of faith, the *shema*: the LORD is our God, the only God, the true and living God. Next the prayer names the characteristics of this mighty God: exists from eternity, remains forever, incomprehensible, absolutely unapproachable. But at the same time this is the Creator God, the source of all life from whom everything comes. He made everything so that his creatures might partake in his holiness, his life, the radiation of which is the light of glory *(doxa, gloria)*. "Source of life and goodness, you have created all things to fill your creatures with every blessing and to lead all of us to the joyful vision of your light. Countless hosts of heaven stand before you to do your will ... united with them and in the name of every creature under heaven we too praise your glory." Then we conclude this part by singing the *Sanctus*, which professes this faith: Holy, holy, holy Lord, God of power and might, heaven and earth are full of your glory." With the angels and the whole of creation we bless and praise God. The first part of Eucharistic Prayer IV thus acknowledges God, as does the first pericope of the *birkat-ha-mazon*.

The second pericope of the Jewish prayer is thanksgiving enumerating the great benefits that God has showered on us throughout salvation history. Likewise, the second part of Eucharistic Prayer IV begins this way: "Father, we acknowledge your greatness ... " *(exomologoumai)*. The Latin text says *confitemur*, its translation of *berakah*. "All your actions show your wisdom and love." Then follows a list of historical events, God's magnificent deeds for us. The prayer leads beautifully through the Old Testament: "You formed us in your own likeness and set us over the whole world to serve you, our Creator and to rule over all creatures. Even when we disobeyed you and lost your friendship ... , you helped all people ... , again and again you offered a covenant to us ... , through the prophets you taught us ... " Next follow the wonderful deeds of the New Testament:

The Liturgy of the Eucharist

"You so loved the world that in the fullness of time you sent your only Son to be our Saviour ... " God's greatest gift to us is the Incarnation, the person of Jesus Christ, the Christ-event. God came among us, became like us, and brought us the Good News of the *Evangelium,* which is summed up here in the text: Christ healed the sick, brought us freedom and consoled everyone. After the historical enumeration comes the crowning event of Christ's life, his death on the cross in loving obedience to the Father. The paschal mystery is presented here, because "by rising from the dead, he destroyed death and restored life." Thus, the second part of this eucharistic prayer, just like the Jewish prayer, is thanksgiving for God's great deeds; the Christian prayer also names the Christ-event, the paschal mystery. We therefore call this part *oratio Christologica*, Christological prayer, through which we arrive at the paschal mystery.

At this point something interesting happens. When the historical account comes to Christ's death on the cross, the Christian tradition inserts into the Jewish prayer structure a special text. "When the time came for him to be glorified ... he took bread ... " This special insertion is called an embolism, that is, a text that was not in the original, but was added from elsewhere. This is nothing other than the gospel account of the Last Supper, concrete, brief, terse and precise.

Not only the account of the Last Supper, but also its logical sequence, the *anamnesis,* is inserted into the structure of the *birkat-hamazon*. The scriptural text ends with the commandment *(mandatum)* of the Lord: "Do this in memory of me," by which the Lord institutes the celebration of the Eucharist until the end of time. The commandment includes the aforementioned words: *anamnesis, memoria,* solemn remembrance. Unfortunately the Greek, Latin, and English translations indicate an intellectual act of remembering something that happened in the past. The original Hebrew word *zikkaron* means much more, a meaning that can also be seen in the Jewish liturgy. In the liturgy of the Jewish paschal meal is a text that reminds the members of the Jewish family who eat the paschal supper, "Keep in mind that, as you now remember the exodus from Egypt, when you eat the paschal lamb in memory of being freed from slavery, not only have your ancestors been freed from the slavery of Egypt, but you and everyone partaking in this ritual are freed from slavery and are being led to God-given freedom." This is the real meaning of *anam-*

nesis. Jesus Christ referred to this when he said to his disciples: "Do this as a memorial for me. Celebrate this symbolic meal, with bread and wine, celebrate it as my memorial-feast." We should not just remember his death on the cross and his resurrection two thousand years ago, but also that all of us who participate in this memorial feast are involved in this past event that now becomes present to us. Therefore, we ought to become active, dynamic participants in the paschal mystery, the paschal transformation, the transition from death to life. The *anamnesis*, therefore, is an invitation to this active, intimate participation by all who take part in the celebration.

The passage of the word *zikkaron* into Greek had another consequence. Translated into Greek for the sake of the Christians in Antioch, the Hebrew and Aramaic *zikkaron* became *anamnesis*, a Greek word meaning simply to remember some past event. It lacked the rich meaning of the Hebrew. Therefore when the Church wanted to say that we obey the Lord's commandment and celebrate his memorial *(anamnesis)*, it always added the word *anaphora (oblatio* in Latin*)*, which means offering or sacrifice in Greek.

Thus in the Greek texts and their translations up to our day, remembrance is always connected to and complemented by *anaphora,* the word of offering, surrender and sacrifice. In the text of Eucharistic Prayer IV, after the Gospel narrative and commandment comes the memorial acclamation, which clearly states that we proclaim the Lord's death and resurrection until he comes again. The text of the *anamnesis* follows immediately: "We now celebrate this memorial of our redemption. We recall Christ's death ... " Remembering is an intellectual act, but at the same time, we also celebrate actively, internally and externally participating in Christ's paschal mystery that will become present through the *anamnesis*. The text of the *anamnesis* indicates that here we deal with offertory, oblation, and self-surrender within the eucharistic sacrifice. Consequently, remembering is not merely an intellectual act, but a deep, inner act in which we are active participants. In the Middle Ages, the eucharistic prayer was called *actio (actio Missae)*. Why? Because we do not simply listen to the Mass, but must become actively involved in Christ's paschal transformation. Through our baptism, we have been invited to this and committed ourselves to live and die with Christ so that we might live with him forever.

The Liturgy of the Eucharist

The text of the *anamnesis* mentions this paschal mystery in detail: "Christ's death, his descent among the dead, his resurrection, and his ascension to your right hand"; his glorious return is also mentioned because it too becomes mysteriously present at this time. In this way we offer sacrificially the Eucharist that Christ has offered once and for all on the cross. It now becomes present for us, that we might all join him, surrendering ourselves to the Father and in Christ making our existential sacrifice.

The eucharistic commandment says: "Do this in memory of me," but St. Paul adds: "Every time you eat this bread and drink this cup, you proclaim the death of the Lord until he comes" (1 Cor 11:25). This already points to the future. On one hand we celebrate the Eucharist as a profession of faith in the central mystery of our faith; on the other hand, we offer it before the Father in supplication, begging for and await the Lord's glorious coming. Thus, through the celebration of the Eucharist we keep alive the expectation of this coming of the Lord, as the ancient Christian acclamation expressed it: *Maranatha!* Come Lord Jesus!

The third pericope of the *birkat-ha-mazon* petitions the Lord to come and be present among us. In Eucharistic Prayer IV, this is how it sounds: "Lord, look upon this sacrifice … " that is, look upon us and accept in your fatherly love this sacrifice. Then, as a sign of your acceptance, send us your Holy Spirit: "By your Holy Spirit, gather all who share this one bread and one cup into the one body of Christ, a living sacrifice of praise." This is the *epiklesis*. It begins by asking the Father to send the Holy Spirit to penetrate everything, especially the sacrificial gifts of bread and wine, and change them into the body and blood of Christ. The newer eucharistic prayers usually express this in the *epiklesis* before the institution narrative. The second *epiklesis* begs that we who receive the body and blood of Christ may be transformed through the working of the Holy Spirit into the mystical Body of Christ. In other words, we ask that the Holy Spirit make us, separate individuals, into the one Body of Christ, the Church. We expect that through his mysterious operation the Holy Spirit may transform both the bread and wine and ourselves into the Body of Christ.

The Jewish prayer asks the Lord to be with us, to come among us, to help us and to build up Jerusalem, the holy city. The eucharistic action reaches its fruit and goal when it arrives at the building up of ecclesial communion (*koinonia*). The eucharistic prayer develops this idea further, introducing the whole Church at this point. We remember all those with whom and for whom we offer this sacrifice: the Holy Father, the Pope, our bishops, priests, the whole people of God, and all those who seek God with a sincere heart. The whole earthly Church is present here, in union *(koinonia)* with the Holy Father and the local bishop. Then we pray for those and with those who died in the peace of Christ: here appears the suffering Church. Finally we remember the victorious Church, the Mother of God, the Blessed Virgin Mary, the apostles and other saints. Thus we express the participation of the saints in heaven in this eucharistic action and communion, and so direct our attention towards heaven. This is the goal of our lives and our eucharistic action, that one day, together with the saints and the whole creation, we might glorify, praise and bless God. At the end of the eucharistic prayer, we bless God with the doxology: "Through [Christ], with him and in him, in the unity of the Holy Spirit, all glory and honour is yours, Almighty Father for ever and ever." To this final *berakah* thunders the response of the created world: "Amen!"

This is the theological and spiritual content of the eucharistic prayer and action in which we find our entire Christian theology and spirituality. But we should not forget that the eucharistic prayer first of all is action, dynamic activity. Done sincerely, with the weight of our whole life behind its words, this hour-long celebration would exhaust our spiritual energy. It is the source of our Christian life and its summit, where we really enter into God's life.

The eucharistic prayer offers a compendium of Christian life: the doctrine of Trinity, our life oriented towards the Father; the mystery of the incarnation, the whole redeeming activity of Jesus Christ. Here we find the whole of salvation history from the creation of the world; we see how the Trinity operates in history and contemplate the mysteries Christ's life presented in the liturgy of the word. We experience the working of the Holy Spirit in the eucharistic action and the outpouring of the Holy Spirit as the fruit of Christ's redeeming work. The Holy Spirit always leads us towards Christ and the Incarnation,

The Liturgy of the Eucharist

and inspires us to be formed and configured to Christ so we can build up the body of Christ which is the Church both here on earth and in heaven. The eucharistic texts also describe the fruits of the working of the Holy Spirit. This transformation also refers to us, for the Holy Spirit transforms individuals into the body of Christ. The liturgy calls this formation of the Church *koinonia*, communion; the ecclesiology of the ancient Church is based on this eucharistic *koinonia*. The Church is present where the faithful gather around the bishop to offer the eucharistic sacrifice. These local churches are connected with one another through the bishop; under the leadership of the Holy Father, they constitute the communion *(koinonia)* of the Church of Christ.

Among the eucharistic gifts of the Holy Spirit is the forgiveness of sins *(aphesis ton hamartion)*. The coming of the Holy Spirit mediates the forgiveness of sins. According to the Council of Trent, the celebration of the Eucharist takes away even the greatest sins. This can be misunderstood if taken to mean that we do not need the sacrament of forgiveness (penance), yet there can be no doubt that according to the liturgical text "the Holy Spirit himself is the forgiveness of sins" *(ipse Spiritus Sanctus est remissio peccatorum)*, provided that we have previously entered into the paschal mystery, that is, have died to ourselves and are now risen.

The eschatological, future-oriented character of the Eucharist is also manifested clearly in our desire to belong to the communion of saints, to go to heaven to praise God with the whole creation. For this reason the Church considers the Eucharist the medicine of immortality *(pharmakon tes athanasias)*, and the bread of eternal life that enables us to live for ever. Another gift of the Holy Spirit in the Eucharist is *parresia:* confidence, trust, boldness. When, at the end of the eucharistic prayer, after the Great Amen, we introduce the Lord's Prayer, we say: "Let us pray with confidence … " The Latin text says: *audemus dicere*, we dare to say Our Father. In other words, we approach the Father with confidence because the gift of *parresia* makes us his children and joins us to the family of God, so that from now on we can say to him: Our Father, our Daddy, our dear father. Here we detect the kind of trust and confidence that a child has in his father: he is not afraid because he knows that his father loves him, defends him and does everything that is good for him. This filial attitude, this boldness is once again the gift of the Holy Spirit through the eucharistic action.

The Mass therefore is an intensive activity. It is not enough just to "hear Mass" or "say Mass." We must be actively involved by exploring and making our own the inner attitudes expressed in the texts. It is important to bring ourselves and include our previous spiritual experiences in the celebration and then, through the words and sacramental actions, express all that is in our hearts. In this way, the eucharistic prayer becomes the compendium of our whole spiritual life.

What kind of spiritual experiences and activities are contained in the eucharistic prayer? First we praise, glorify, bless God. We can do this only if we love life, the Creator, and our dependence on the Creator, which is not easy, especially when we are beset with troubles. To acknowledge God's greatness and goodness and, at the same time, to sacrifice our life on these occasions, requires spiritual strength. The same can be said about thanksgiving. We ought to bring to the Mass all that has happened during our salvation-history: private life, family, nation, each with its own salvation history through which God leads us, often on crooked ways, but always with fatherly care. Such a historical recollection of our past life enables us to discover God's marvellous deeds. We ought to bring to Mass everything that happens in our spiritual life, the events of the past day or week, its sorrows and joys, and give thanks for them all. The Eucharist also provides for us a place to beg, especially when we feel our weak, creaturely, sinful selves. Realizing that we cannot stand alone or live without God's help, we beg and entreat God to be with us at every moment of our pilgrim way.

Active participation in the Mass also demands that we take the threefold dimension of the liturgical signs and symbols seriously. The divine action of the past becomes present now, so that I can enjoy it, and it points to the future where I long to go. Like the early Christians who insistently prayed for the coming of the Lord in their acclamation, we should include this longing in the Mass: *"Maranatha!"* "Come Lord Jesus!"

Our Eucharistic celebration is also a meal, an *agape*, a sober and dignified sacrificial meal. The meal symbolism makes us aware of

The Liturgy of the Eucharist

our union of love with Christ and with one another, so that it can produce that unity, communion *(koinonia),* which is the Church. This joyful meal lets us receive the Bread of Life every day. The primitive Church called this daily communion, *Viaticum (ephodion),* because it was truly food for our pilgrim journey. This clearly opposes the Jansenist opinion, according to which only truly holy people may receive communion. This is not the right Christian attitude. The Lord gave the Eucharist to us sinners to strengthen us for our daily life.

We should bring our daily prayer life to the Mass where it is joined to the great, transformative action of Christ. By keeping us from withdrawing into our individual sorrows and woes, and letting us share them with others, the Mass widens our horizons and makes us truly "catholic," having universal interests. Here the whole Church prays and celebrates; here we deal with the interests and needs of the whole Church. Our Christian life opens up in time and space. This broader, catholic aspect of the Mass is served also by the feasts of the saints, when we realize our solidarity with the great figures and the great multitudes of ordinary Christians of our past and in the celebration of the Eucharist. Nor do we forget the cosmos. In the Oriental liturgy this is much more prevalent. In the Western church, we are so awed by redemption that we have almost forgotten creation and its rich variety of gifts. Yet, redemption cannot be considered independently from creation. In Sunday Mass we ought to pay more attention to the beauty of creation and the greatness of the Creator! Sunday is not only the celebration of the resurrection, but also of creation. This presupposes that we accept the beauty and goodness of creation and rejoice in it.

Having explored the central aspect of our eucharistic celebration, the eucharistic prayer, we now turn briefly to other parts of the liturgy of the Mass.

First, the entrance rites. Some kind of preparation is necessary so we can celebrate Mass with interior participation. We need to concentrate so we can recognize what we're going to do and what will happen during the sacred action that follows.

We begin with the entrance procession. The Mass has four processions: the entrance, the offertory, the communion and the recessional processions. The meaning of the entrance and recessional processions is quite clear, but it is worthwhile noting that the entrance antiphon does not have to be recited by the priest or the people if there is no procession or accompanying singing. The offertory procession has meaning only if there is a real procession, well organized ahead of time, with persons appointed to carry the bread and wine and the collected money to the altar. Of course this procession too, ought to be accompanied with singing. The communion procession has it own antiphon which again does not need to be read if it is not sung.

As the Mass begins, the priest kisses the altar, expressing his love for Jesus Christ, because the altar symbolizes Christ. After the sign of the cross, the priest greets the people with one of the scriptural forms given in the sacramentary (not with a casual good morning). Here the priest should say a few words tailored to the occasion and circumstances to introduce the celebration of the day, and make contact with the people. This is not a homily, but a simple, intimate introduction to the celebration of the liturgy. It might point briefly to the scriptural readings, refer to the liturgical season or the saint of the day, take a pointer that indicates the tone of the celebration from the text of the entrance antiphon, or highlight an element or two from the rich mystery of the Eucharist.

The penitential prayer is merely a brief reminder of our own unworthiness and sinfulness, and of God's great mercy. This is not the time for a detailed examination of conscience.

For a lengthier treatment of the liturgy of the word, see chapter 8. The homily focuses on the image of Christ that appears in the daily gospel, making it an experiential event for the people. The same Christ who appears in the gospels as a Good Shepherd, as Saviour carrying the cross, or as the miracle-working Jesus appears even more concretely and tangibly in the Mass under the species of bread and wine.

Next follows the preparation of the gifts for the sacrificial offering that happens later in the eucharistic prayer. Here the gifts of bread and wine are laid on the altar to the accompaniment of some prayers of blessing (*berakah*) taken from the Jewish liturgy. We should not simply put money into the collection basket; we should also be ready to offer ourselves on the altar, to be transformed together with Christ. The washing of the hands, originally meant to be a real cleansing of

The Liturgy of the Eucharist

the hands after handling and selecting the gifts, now symbolizes that we should approach the eucharistic offering with pure hearts and minds.

After the Great Amen of the eucharistic prayer comes the communion rite. First, in the Lord's prayer, the family prayer of the Christian community, we express our filial relationship to God. The embolism: "Deliver us, Lord, from every evil ... ," simply expands the last petition of the Lord's Prayer and should be understood in an eschatological perspective. In other words, it looks ahead to the last judgment and asks the Lord to free us from every evil when we stand in front of his throne at the judgment. The annexed doxology, "For the kingdom, the power, and the glory are yours ... " is not of Protestant origin—it was already present at the end of first-century liturgical texts. It too has eschatological significance.

The kiss of peace is an ancient Christian custom that can already be found in the New Testament writings. We may have had some practical problems in implementing it because we were unaccustomed to such intimate greetings, especially in cities where the faithful hardly know each other. In some places the people turn towards each other not merely with a simple handshake, but with a more intimate double handshake as they exchange the peace. Yet, this gesture beautifully expresses the essence of any ecclesial community, our belonging together. What does this peace mean here? Among the first Christians the Greek word *eirene* (in Latin *pax*) means almost the same thing as *koinonia*, that is, union and communion with Christ and with one another. Whenever we say "Peace be with you!," or when we see the word "Pax" on tombstones, it does not mean that the deceased can be left in peace because nobody is disturbing them any more. Rather it means that even if the person has died, our union, our communion *(koinonia)* in Jesus Christ abides. The expression of this communion and peace is the kiss of peace. It may receive a somewhat different meaning when it is used at the end of the penitential liturgy; in this case the kiss of peace is the sign of reconciliation, that is, of the restoration of unity and communion. Shared before holy communion, the kiss of peace expresses that inner union among us which is the prelude to the reception of holy communion. Such an inner communion does not mean uniformity, but unity in diversity.

The practical implementation of this beautiful ancient Christian custom requires great pastoral prudence.

After the kiss of peace comes the breaking of the bread, which has been neglected in the Latin liturgy. Even today, we do it rather minimally, especially when we use a thin white wafer for bread. Yet the breaking of the bread has deep biblical roots. The time may come when we will be able to solve the practical difficulties connected with this, and use real, though unleavened bread according to the custom of the Western Church, but bread that looks like real bread, breaks like bread, is broken and tastes like bread. Its liturgical symbolism would be stronger; the meaning of the breaking of bread would also be better highlighted; we break the one bread and we all participate in that one (loaf of) bread.

It is important to pay attention to the fact that people should always receive holy communion from bread (or hosts) consecrated at that Mass. Only in the case of true necessity, when it is difficult to determine ahead of time the number of communicants, should we have recourse to the Eucharist preserved in the tabernacle. During the breaking of the bread we should sing the Agnus Dei, which accompanies the breaking and at the same time prepares us for holy communion.

Though Jesus Christ is truly and completely present under the species of bread alone, the Lord's commandment is better fulfilled if we both eat his body and drink his blood. Communion under both species, which the Church allows in certain cases, is therefore more complete from a liturgical viewpoint. If the distribution of holy communion is well prepared, that is, if there are enough chalices and ministers of communion, then this should not create problems, or unduly prolong the distribution.

In many places, the faithful receive the Eucharist not on their tongue, but in their hand. This is a return to the ancient Christian custom practised up until about the seventh century. Both forms are acceptable, both should be carried out with reverence. Sometimes the priest leaves the paten or ciborium on the altar, and the people go up and take the host themselves. As a liturgical practice, this is wrong. One of the important symbolic actions of the Eucharist is that

The Liturgy of the Eucharist

someone gives it to us; it is not self-service. The Lord Jesus gives himself to us; the minister of communion (priest, deacon or appointed lay person) represents Christ himself in giving. The words, "The body of Christ" and "The blood of Christ" invite us to profess our faith in the Eucharist as we say "Amen." Therefore we don't say, "Come and get it." Rather we distribute it; we give Christ's body and blood. Thus the distribution of communion becomes the symbolic expression of giving, surrendering, handing over ourselves for the sake of others.

Once holy communion is over and the vessels are set aside for later purification, we spend a few minutes in silence in order to deepen the meaning of our wondrous communion with Christ and one another. This silence should help us savour our belonging to the eucharistic community and appreciate our individual intimate relationship with Christ. It is quite possible to look around "in holy distraction" and delight in seeing the other Christians with whom, together, we form the family of God and Church of Jesus Christ.

Following the silence, the prayer after communion sums up our thanksgiving. Then there is place for announcements that reflect the life of the local parish. Finally the priest blesses the people, asking the Lord for the necessary gifts. Sometimes on Sunday we should use the triple blessing which the 1970 Sacramentary introduced into the Roman liturgy from the Mozarabic rite. The dismissal itself is actually a send-off. The Mass is over, now go in peace, in the peace of Christ, and put into practice in your everyday life all that you have celebrated here—because from now on you have to live accordingly. You have to live out eucharistic communion, love, surrender, obedience to the Father's will, union with Christ, the paschal mystery, and the miracle of the indwelling of the Holy Spirit in your heart.

Chapter 12

THE LITURGY OF FORGIVENESS AND RECONCILIATION

The revision of the ritual books shows perhaps the greatest modification in the case of the liturgy of forgiveness (Penance). Not only are the external forms altered, but the Church expects people to change their whole attitude towards the sacrament. Already the name given to this sacrament by the Church today indicates that here we are dealing not only with penance, but also with reconciliation. Throughout history this sacrament has been called by different names: sacrament of penance, of contrition, of confession, of forgiveness, and now, of reconciliation. In our day the Church prefers to talk about reconciliation, though "penance" is still the commonly used title. It is important to note that reconciliation means more than the forgiveness and taking away of our sins. Reconciliation means something positive, the restoration and deepening of our union and communion with God.

Another terminological change is evident. People often say in connection with this sacrament that "I'm going to confession," or "I'm going to hear confessions," although confession is only part of the sacramental process. Rather, we ought to say that we are going to celebrate the sacrament of reconciliation, because in reality we are dealing here with celebration, too. Every liturgy— even the funeral and penance liturgies—is a feast. To celebrate means to take part gladly, joyfully, in that communal action, where we enter into a dialogue with God. This kind of attitude is a bit different from the one that dominated the second thousand years of Christianity, when we saw in the Sacrament of Penance only a sad walk through a cemetery, where we beat our breast with long faces and, after a painful examination of conscience, whispered our sins in confession, which concluded with absolution.

A brief look at the history of the sacrament of penance will make many things more understandable.

Here, as in every sacrament, we are dealing with a process. The sacramental liturgy is not just a momentary event, but a longer process. In the first centuries this process may have lasted for years. According to ancient liturgical sources, someone who had committed a grave sin, and then, moved by the grace of God, repented and wanted to turn back to God, had to go first to the bishop or priest, and tell him those sins by which he had offended God and the community. The bishop received the penitent with kindness, and after he was convinced of the sincerity of the penitent's conversion, imposed on him a certain penance for a definite time as a proof of the sincerity of his conversion. In some cases this period of doing penance lasted for ten to twenty years; during this time penitents had to fast, wear sackcloth and pray a lot. They could not receive holy communion, but could participate in the liturgy of the word. In a certain sense, this was a "salutary excommunication"; penitents were excluded for one purpose: becoming aware of their sinful behaviour would awaken in them the desire for eucharistic communion with the Church. Once the time of penance was over—normally on Holy Thursday, the bishop, in the presence of the whole community, received the penitents back again into the eucharistic community by the imposition of hands and a supplicatory prayer. Everyone rejoiced and embraced the converted penitents: prodigal sons and daughters who had been lost had returned home again, and could now participate in the eucharistic banquet again. This practice of roughly the first thousand years, with its heavy penitential discipline, was made even more serious since the sacrament of forgiveness could be received only once in a lifetime.

The process of forgiving sins always has four elements. First, sinners are touched by God's grace and convert. Second, they confess their sins. Third, they perform the penance imposed on them, and accept their salutary excommunication. The fourth and final element is the liturgical celebration of the whole process with the imposition of hands and prayer of absolution.

The Liturgy of Forgiveness and Reconciliation

This structure of the sacramental process was somewhat altered with the introduction of private confession, which first began in the seventh century in Ireland. From there it gradually spread to the continent of Europe, until finally, around the turn of the millennium, it became a universal practice. What did this change mean? First of all, the faithful could go to confession, not just once in a lifetime, but more often. They could receive sacramental absolution not only for grave sin, but also for venial sins. The penance imposed was also modified and lightened. The most significant change, however, was that after true contrition and confession, penitents could receive absolution right away, and do their penance later. This became the penitential practice of the second thousand years, which is still in usage.

Today, as we begin the third millennium, the renewed rite of the sacrament of forgiveness suggests another structural change. There is no question that the first and most important element in the penitential process is always conversion, contrition (*metanoia*), reconciliation with God in the depth of our hearts. It is possible now, that after such heartfelt contrition, people receive absolution immediately. The revised ritual offers this possibility and, in certain circumstances, it also allows "general absolution" as a possible form of the sacrament. Without private confession, within a communal penitential liturgy, after a communal general confession of sins, penitents may receive general absolution. Even grave sins can be forgiven in this way, but penitents who are conscious of grave sins must confess these sins later in private confession and perform the imposed penance.

What is happening here? Among the four essential elements of the penitential process in the first thousand years, absolution was in fourth place; in the second thousand years it moved ahead to third place, and it seems that in the third millennium it may advance even further to second place, right after contrition. The current change therefore is not unheard of, since similar changes have happened already. The Church has the power to change the structure and discipline of the sacrament according to the needs of the faithful, provided that the essence of the sacrament remains the same.

This brief historical overview points out that, among the four essential elements, every age emphasized the element that immediately preceded sacramental absolution. In the first thousand years, when liturgical absolution was in last place, the performance of penance preceded it immediately; consequently penance was emphasized. It took a long time to perform the imposed penance and arrive at the moment of absolution. Even the theological reflections of that age dealt mostly with the subject of doing penance, proving its importance, and elaborating on the different kinds of penances for different kinds of sins (tariff penance). A similar thing happened in the second thousand years. When absolution moved ahead to third place, the element that immediately preceded it was the confession of sins. Hence, theologians emphasized the importance of confession. The sacrament itself was called "the sacrament of confession," and we spoke about going to confession, etc., when we wanted to receive the sacrament. Thus, confession seemed to be most important in the whole process. Our catechisms were preoccupied with teaching people how to make a complete, detailed confession, enumerating their sins according to number, species, and circumstances. If these observations are right, when a new period begins, and general absolution arrives in second place, the greatest emphasis will have to be laid on the first element, conversion and contrition, whereby sinners turn back again to God and abandon the ways of sin. Our theological reflection, catechesis and pastoral activity should now be directed to making contrition and conversion the centre of the sacramental process. This means we should explore what it means to "convert." How can we make this inner change as we listen to the word of God? How can we cooperate with divine grace and turn to God in all sincerity?

The history of the sacrament of penance shows the four elements of the process. No matter how we change their order, the four elements must always be present. If one is missing, then the sacramental process is not complete. Even if we receive general absolution right after contrition, people still have to go to confession and do penance to complete the process.

The four constant elements of the penitential process are contrition, confession, satisfaction and absolution. According to the teaching of the catechism (cf. CCC 1451), in the act of contrition we repent of our sins, turn from sin to God, acknowledge with sorrow that we have offended God, and firmly promise to not sin again. This is a conversion! If at the root of every sin is a failure to acknowledge

God as God, then conversion will consist precisely in recognizing that God is the "only God," the Almighty who is also Father. With contrition we open ourselves before God; we bless, praise and love God, and subject ourselves to his will. While this conversion could be approached theologically, psychologically and sociologically, I will look at three moments that should be present in every act of contrition.

The first of these moments refers to the past. Often we may be sorry for our sins, but we resent and cannot "forgive" God who let us sin. We resent God because he allowed this to happen to us. When we want to truly repent, we must also be able to forgive God for letting us fail. In other words, we have to accept our past, even if the road was rather crooked, because we believe that God can bring something good out of it. To those who love God everything serves for their own good! And so we apply a healing balm to the wounds of our past when we repent.

In this process the present is transformed. After sincere repentance, the good God, in his infinite mercy, loves us more (to use an anthropomorphic expression) than before. God's mercy, so wonderful and mysterious, makes us more precious after our repentance than before we sinned. Human justice can hardly understand this, but this is a mystery of faith, the mystery of God's mercy that can bring good even out of sin, and for whom the grace of redemption is more powerful and more beautiful than the gift of creation. We don't have to start everything anew or begin where we were before we sinned. God's mercy is so immense and superabundant that after we have sinned and repented, the Lord raises us higher than we were before. We can only accept this mystery in faith—humbly and gratefully.

The act of contrition also looks to the future: to accepting the possibility that we may sin again. Pastoral practice indicates that this creates a significant problem, especially for young people who do not want to be hypocrites. Unable to unconditionally promise that they will sin no more, they would rather not go to the sacraments. The Church never expected someone would be canonized after celebrating reconciliation; the Church simply requires merely that when we express our love for God in contrition, we do not say: "I love you, God, but I am going to sin again and I will offend you again." Such a love would not be true contrition. True contrition does not exclude the insight, gained from experience, that probably we will fail again, although we would love to avoid it. Even the saints failed several times daily, we are told. From experience we know very well that we are sinners, stumbling pilgrims on the road of our earthly pilgrimage. For this reason our act of contrition has to humbly accept that we may sin again in the future. When this happens we will know immediately what we have to do: get up and run to the merciful, crucified Jesus, asking to be forgiven and welcomed back into his arms once more. The greatest tragedy is not that we fall, but that we remain on the ground!

The second constant element of the penitential process is confession, which expresses the sincerity of our conversion. It manifests our sincere desire for healing. It is not enough to speak about healing in generalities; we have to point concretely to our wounds and pain. When we see a doctor, the doctor's first question will be, "Where does it hurt, your head or your foot?" Certain psychological problems in relation to a detailed and complete (integral) confession may emerge, especially in the younger generation. Yet, one can and should expect penitents to indicate the areas in which they are experiencing difficulties. The integrity of confession is of such great value that we must not neglect or abandon it. But neither should we kill the good intention of the penitent with overzealous insistence on integrity. Practise it with pastoral prudence insofar as it helps the penitent— and in many cases it does. Ask questions to detect not only the symptoms, but also the causes of the sickness, but do not try to love the penitent to death, bothering them in the name of integrity. The virtue of pastoral prudence is extremely important here. At the same time, the Church has the obligation to care for those who have separated themselves, by their grave sin, from the kingdom of God. It is the Church's duty to stand by these penitents and help them in the healing that leads them home. To not be concerned with integrity would constitute pastoral negligence because the Church has received from Christ the mission to propagate and defend the kingdom of God, and direct penitents on the road towards it.

The third element of the penitential process is satisfaction, or doing penance. Rather than look on this as a penalty or reparation, the new rite favours a much more medicinal approach to help sick

The Liturgy of Forgiveness and Reconciliation

persons move towards healing, turn from the wrong way, and learn how to walk the right road.

Finally a few words about absolution, the most liturgical element in the whole process, which therefore should be surrounded by sacramental and liturgical symbols, as the rite suggests. Absolution is accompanied by the laying on of hands, by which the Holy Spirit is called down on and conferred on the penitent. According to the liturgy of the Church, the Holy Spirit is the remission of our sins; in other words, the sacrament drives away the spirit of evil from our heart, and the Holy Spirit returns to take up his dwelling place in it again. This is truly a Pentecost event! The text of the prayer of absolution clearly cites and makes present the paschal mystery. Penitents are immersed into the death and resurrection of Christ when they die to themselves and their self-centredness, and come to new life in Jesus Christ.

There are two ways to consider the sacrament of reconciliation: on one hand, as the sacrament of resurrection, necessary for all those who have severed their relationship with God through grave sin. This best manifests the paschal mystery: the sinner is raised up to new life. On the other hand, according to the thousand-year tradition of the Church, the sacrament can also be seen as the special form of forgiving venial sins. Venial sins can be forgiven in manifold ways. The faithful don't seem to know this very well; today many think that venial sins can be forgiven only through confession. Christians in the early centuries were quite aware of the fact that venial sins are forgiven in many ways: sincerely praying the Lord's Prayer, which the early Christians considered almost a sacrament, is but one example! Other activities that forgive sin include participating in the Eucharist, rekindling the virtues of faith, hope and charity, engaging in acts of charity and different devotions, saying the act of contrition in the examination of conscience, etc. Done out of love for God, all these may merit forgiveness for us. The sacrament of forgiveness is therefore not the only way to gain forgiveness for venial sins; it is a privileged form of this forgiveness, celebrated with some liturgical formality. In such occasions we can speak of rejuvenation or healing, and the sacrament can be called the sacrament of healing.

According to the new rite, the sacrament of reconciliation can be celebrated in three ways. The first is individual celebration, with only the penitent and the priest taking part. The Church still considers this the regular celebration of the sacrament, but at the same time wants us to celebrate it according to new ideas. The new rite directs our attention to the right concept of sin, to the many possibilities of receiving forgiveness, to the social effects of sin and the ecclesial character of forgiveness. Here, as in the other sacraments, the Church wishes to give a larger role to the word of God, even when it is celebrated privately. Unfortunately, we are not sufficiently prepared to do this; we do not know the Bible well enough to be able to cite or suggest or read a relevant passage from it on a given occasion. We should be more convinced that the word of God works more forcefully than any smart human counselling. Furthermore, we cannot consider that we merely administer this sacrament: someone enters the confessional or the penitential room, recites their sins, almost automatically gets absolution and then leaves. The spirit of the celebration requires all this to happen in a prayerful atmosphere. Penitents should be received amicably by the priest, just as Christ received sinners whom he came to heal and for whom he gave his life. During the conversation, penitents should have the opportunity to tell freely and calmly how they stand before God. Even better, they can describe how they live up to their baptismal, marriage, priestly, religious vows. This conversation ought to happen in an atmosphere in which penitents can open their hearts confidently. This humane conversation is part of the celebration, just like the (epicletic) prayer when the penitent (perhaps together with the confessor) kneels to ask the Father and the crucified Christ for the forgiveness of sins, so that the Church of Christ may become more and more his immaculate Bride. Absolution follows, with the "epicletic" laying on of hands and the rich text that we mentioned earlier. Finally, the celebration concludes with thanksgiving: We give praise to the almighty God and heavenly Father, the One God, whose mercy not only the penitent, but also the priest and the whole church experienced. Thus, even individual confession is a real liturgical celebration.

Of course, such celebrations take more time! Consequently, in the future we may not have the opportunity to go to confession as often as we did in the past. Therefore the Church recommends two other liturgical ways of celebrating the forgiveness of sins.

The second liturgical form of the sacrament of forgiveness is the communal penitential service which may be followed by individual confessions and absolutions, if enough confessors are available. The penitential liturgy in this case is nothing other than a liturgy of the word with biblical texts that inspire repentance, homily, songs and prayers. All this awakens true contrition, through which the faithful then can find forgiveness for their venial sins. An opportunity for individual confession provides first of all for the forgiveness of grave sins, but obviously for other sins as well.

In such cases, however, there is a danger that, because of the great number of penitents, everything happens fast, and the celebrative character of the sacrament will be lost. In current circumstances, the combination of communal and individual celebration can be an important transition because it emphasizes both the communal and personal character of the sacrament.

The third liturgical form of the sacrament of forgiveness is a communal penitential liturgy with general absolution. With the permission of the Episcopal Conference and the local bishop, this can be allowed only when so many people wish to receive the sacrament that the available priests would not, within a reasonable time, be able to assure that everyone would be able to celebrate reconciliation according to the renewed spirit we have just discussed. In such cases, within the framework of a communal liturgy, all those who repent of their sins with true contrition and somehow manifest their desire to be absolved may receive it in general absolution. Those who are conscious only of venial sins gain forgiveness through sacramental (general) absolution, after they have confessed their common sinfulness, and participated in the prayers of penance of the communal liturgy. Those who are conscious of grave sins gain full forgiveness through general absolution, but must go to individual confession whenever there is an opportunity in the near future, accept the spiritual counselling for the restoration of their spiritual life, and the due penance imposed on them. (In such a delayed confession, it is not necessary to give and receive absolution, since the penitent's sins have already been forgiven by the general absolution; if the penitent asks for it, the confessor may give it on the basis of the penitent's contrite heart.) This belated confession and penance are necessary, as we have said before, because only in this way does the sacramental process become complete. Only in this way can the Church fulfil the commission she received from Christ: that she stand by and help her errant and sick children.

Such penitential liturgies with general absolution may become more frequent in the future, but right now, few dioceses use them. The problem is that we are not sufficiently prepared for it. Our way of thinking, our attitude does not yet mirror the spirit of the new liturgy. We ought to pay more attention to the word of God that calls us to repentance; be more aware of the different forms of forgiveness; more frequently participate in penitential liturgies, and prepare ourselves more sincerely for the celebration of the sacrament, though these are less frequent than in the past. In particular, we ought to make our own the true spirit of conversion. All this still lies in the future. But if it happens, it is easy to imagine that, after a generation or so, general absolution will become more available—two or three times a year, especially in Advent and Lent. There the faithful will be able to receive sacramental absolution for the forgiveness of their sins. However, at least once a year people should celebrate the sacrament in a way that they personally give an account of themselves and the state of their Christian life to the Church and to their God.

Chapter 13

THE LITURGY OF THE ANOINTING OF THE SICK

One of the important aspects of pastoral activity is to care for the flock, especially those who are sick, poor and abandoned. Sooner or later sickness touches every one of us; we all arrive one day at the point when, either as the result of old age or some ailment, our strength begins to fail and we have to prepare for the transition of death. Earlier I mentioned how important it is to have a truly Christian view of death. Christians should not look on it as a tragedy, but as the crowning of our life for which we ought to prepare ourselves in expectation. In that moment alone we will be able to surrender ourselves into God's hands, freely, consciously and with the loving obedience that we promised at our baptism and tried to practice throughout our whole life. Only then can we truly be open towards our Almighty God and Father and truly participate perfectly in the paschal mystery according to our human capacity. It is worthwhile thinking and speaking more often about this paschal transformation that happens at death. The spiritual and pastoral care of the sick, and the anointing of the sick will hardly be fruitful if we do not prepare them for that moment. It is our duty while we are still healthy to meditate upon the Christian meaning of sickness, suffering, old age and death.

The revised rite deals not only with the sacrament of anointing, but also with the spiritual care of the sick. In other words, the care of the sick is not restricted to only one visit when we anoint the sick person to prepare them in some magic way to enter heaven. Here too is a sacramental process that consists of preparation, celebration and then practical implementation in everyday life. First, the rite insists that we visit the sick. This is a Christian mission. Jesus Christ went around doing good, helping the downtrodden, healing the sick, and sometimes even raising the dead. During his earthly life, he sent his apostles with this mission. The Church continues this mission when she cares for the sick.

We already mentioned that it is a primary task of the priest to care for his flock, especially the lost, straying, wounded sheep. Alone he is unable to do this, and he may not have enough time along with his other tasks. For this reason he needs laypeople who can assume this ministry of regularly visiting the sick. This is so important in the eyes of the Church that it recently allowed laypeople to take the Blessed Sacrament to the sick again, at least once a week, especially on Sundays, and daily if possible. Alone the priest would be unable to do this, especially in big cities where people are so scattered. Yet the Church wants to care for its sick members, to assure them that in their sickness they are still important members of the parish, the local church and the whole Church. All Christians are called to support them with our prayers, but also in other ways, especially by sharing with them the sacramental presence of the Lord. When they visit the sick, visitors should chat with the sick people, encourage them, pray together, read from the Bible, etc. The Church's care should also be manifest in sacramental forms, such as offering them the possibility of celebrating the sacrament of forgiveness when the priest has an opportunity to visit them.

A special sacramental form of the care of the sick is the sacrament of anointing. Since Vatican II, we call this, not the sacrament of the dying but the sacrament of the sick, since it is first of all for the sick. Only exceptionally—when there was no opportunity to receive it sooner—is it for the dying. So they are prepared to celebrate it fruitfully, the Church wants sick people to be anointed when they still have full use of their minds. They should be able to perceive the meaning of the liturgical symbols and listen to the word of God and so be strengthened through the sacramental anointing and the prayer of faith. The proper fruit of anointing is healing, not only the healing of the body, but also of the soul, of the whole person. The word "healing" has a double meaning in Greek (*sotéria, salus*): physical healing and salvation. According to Christian teaching, salvation means not only physical health, but primarily, the way to reach full salvation, that is, heaven. Anointing is not a sacrament that heals all physical sickness; rather, it makes us "whole," capable of salvation. If the sacrament had some magical effect, then we could just ask for it when we felt weak, and continue to live on earth for thousands of years. But who wants to stay here for thousands of years? We long for salvation, for harmony of body and soul, for peace with God and all people, and in this sense for "health" (*salus*). In every sickness, as in old age, the problem is that a split occurs among the different faculties and relations: between body and soul, in relation to oneself, to God and to others. Harmony, wholeness, "health" is disturbed. The proper effect of the sacrament is to restore this wholeness, this harmony. In other words, sick people will be able to integrate their sickness, rather than letting it be a source of alienation. In this way sick people accept themselves.

The sacrament of anointing can be given only to those who are seriously ill, not in some trivial sickness such as the flu or a nosebleed. The sickness is supposed to be such that it can lead to death if not attended to medically. The sacrament could be given to those who face surgery, even an appendectomy, nowadays considered a simple routine operation. But without surgery, someone who has appendicitis could die in a short time; thus, conferring of the sacrament is justified before such a surgery, especially if anesthetics are administered. Anesthesia generally affects the sick person quite deeply. The seriousness of the sickness should be judged not only objectively, that is, according to the medical data, but also subjectively: how does it affect the sick person? We ought to take into account how much such a medical intervention disturbs the patient. The healing effect of the sacrament is designed to calm the sick people and enable them to integrate their sickness and its consequences into their lives in a Christian way.

Receiving the sacrament is also justified when old age disturbs our spiritual balance, our relationship to God and to others; when we begin to fail: we cannot read or walk, etc. In these situations we really need the grace of the sacrament.

The sacrament of anointing is for those who suffer some kind of physical illness. It is not for those who are sick spiritually, or have some psychological disorder: for them, the sacrament of forgiveness, which also has a healing effect, is more appropriate. Though it is not easy to separate the physical and spiritual components of a sickness, the sacramental sign of anointing refers more to bodily illness than to those of the spiritual. At a congress of psychologists and theologians a few years ago, this problem was discussed. Participants concluded that psychological illnesses in themselves do not mean danger of death (except in the case of manic depression).

Therefore, the sacrament of forgiveness with imposition of hands would be more apt to heal psychological sickness than the anointing of the sick.

Since anointing is the sacrament of the sick, it is not right to use it for healthy people. It has happened that a priest told his people: "Since we are all sick for one reason or other, everyone should come to receive the sacrament of anointing." This is a kind of abuse of the true meaning of the sacrament. It is perhaps useful to mention here that charismatic groups use blessed (not consecrated) oil. This anointing with the blessed oil is not a sacrament, but a sacramental, with its own special blessing in the ritual. Charismatics often use this oil for various purposes. We ought to be careful not to confuse the two.

The ritual indicates those whom the doctors have already declared dead are not anointed: "If the sick person to whom the priest is called has died already, the priest should pray for him that the Lord may forgive his sins and receive him into his kingdom. But he should not give the anointing to the deceased." Here again people will need some instruction. They need to understand that because the sacrament is for the sick, sick people should celebrate it before they have lost consciousness. To stress this point, it may be advisable to omit this sacrament at the moment of death. The sacrament of dying is not anointing, but the Viaticum, the Eucharist. When the priest is called to the bedside of someone who is already clinically dead, he should not anoint them. Rather he should sign the deceased with the sign of the cross on the forehead and say the prayers of the dying, but not anoint the person, because the sacrament does not have some magic power. Sacraments can be given only to living persons who can still, in some minimal way, perceive the words and symbols of the sacrament.

In the case of a chronic illness such as chronic arthritis, blindness, deafness, etc., the sacrament can be administered. Because such illnesses seriously disturb a person's inner composure, they very much need the sacrament's healing grace.

It is important to prepare the sick person for the sacrament. We have to take care to explain, not just the rite itself, but also what they receive through it: "healing" in its full sense and sanctifying grace that can be best illustrated by our relationship to the three divine Persons. Our loving obedience towards the Father is strengthened insofar as we accept the will of the One who can do with us whatever he wants. While he may send us sickness, allow us to grow old and weak, we still trust in him and can utter, "Your will be done, not mine!" Our relationship to Jesus Christ in this sacrament consists in our union with his life, since we have been baptized into his life, suffering and death. Therefore we live this period of suffering with him, and united with him we contribute to what is still missing in his body, the Church. Then from the Holy Spirit we expect the gift that fills us with confidence and even joy, that we might now be more like Christ, and give witness to others about the relevance of the paschal mystery.

When the Church surrounds the sick with her sacraments, she wants to assure them that they are not left alone. The grace of anointing consoles the sick in their loneliness. It is well known that in sickness everyone becomes a little bit selfish; the sacrament helps us break out of this self-centredness, and perhaps even makes us altruistic when it assures us of the presence and care of the Church. In the persons of the visitors of the sick, the parish-community, the nurses and doctors, and the priest, the Church stands beside the sick person. It is important to tell this to those who are sick, since when people approach the final sacrifice of their life, they are entering the most important period of their life. At this time they should not feel alone or abandoned, but should be assured of the presence of others, of the Church.

The rite of the sacrament of anointing is quite simple and clear. In the beginning there is the renewal of sorrow for our sins, or perhaps even a celebration of the sacrament of reconciliation. The liturgy of the word follows, adapted to the circumstances. Ideally the anointing takes place in the midst of the family, perhaps with the participation of nurses (and doctors?). It is rather difficult to do this in the hospital, where the celebration necessarily has to be shortened. It is also possible to celebrate the anointing in a church or chapel, especially if we want to anoint several sick persons together. If this happens in the presence of the whole parish community, it would be even more effective for both the sick and the faithful. It would be advisable to have such a communal celebration of anointing once or twice a year, but it has to be well prepared ahead of time. When sick people are transported to the church in wheelchairs or on stretchers, doctors and nurses should be involved with the whole parish in the celebration. Common celebrations allow them to experience how closely the whole community accompanies them with their prayers and support.

Let us consider briefly the liturgical symbols of the sacrament. For the anointing, the oil of the sick, which was blessed by the bishop at the Mass of Chrism where the priests and people of the whole diocese gathered, is used. People should know the origin of the holy oil. In many places the priest takes home the blessed oil and solemnly shows it to the people in his parish church before the evening Mass of the Last Supper. He explains to them that all oil used at baptism, confirmation, anointing of the sick, and ordination comes from the paschal mystery through the bishop's blessing. Normally olive oil is used, but other vegetable oils are also permitted. It would be worth experimenting with other oils because olive oil is not the most preferable today.

The Church used olive oil because it was normally used in the East, but today it would perhaps be more advisable to use another more highly-scented oil, such as rose oil (attar) to highlight the soothing, healing effect of the oil. In ancient times people anointed the ailing parts of the sick person's body with oil to soothe their pain. Even today in the hospitals the staff uses scented baby oil for soothing and refreshing an aching body. The natural reason for anointing consists in soothing, refreshing and healing; we should pay attention to this since we receive healing grace through the symbols. They ought to express clearly what happens here: the healing, caressing, refreshing love of God is now touching the body of the sick person. The sacramental gesture ought to be this caressing touch. When in the Middle Ages our liturgy became overly ritualized, this caressing gesture became a simple sign of the cross on the forehead of the sick. Even now we anoint the sick in this way: we dip our finger into a small container and draw a sign of the cross on the forehead and hands of the sick. It would be better to keep the holy scented oil in a larger container into which we could dip a few fingers. We could then anoint the forehead and hands of the sick person with soothing, caressing movements. This would better express that here and now, Christ's healing love touches the sick.

According to the Letter of James, the essential part of the sacrament of anointing is the prayer of faith that will heal, save, raise up the sick person through the anointing with the holy oil. The Letter of James indicates clearly that, besides the anointing with oil, the prayer of faith heals the sick person. Perhaps we did not pay enough attention to this prayer of faith. This means that the whole Church, the whole parish community, is represented in the person of the priest. Together, with faith, they all pray insistently for this person's healing. The "prayer of faith" is not just the recitation of the sacramental formula, but also the sincere petition that the priest, the sick person, and the faithful who are present say in the depths of their hearts.

As in the other sacraments, the *epiklesis* is present here. The silent imposition of hands symbolizes the asking for and conferring of the grace of the Holy Spirit. Another pentecost event! The laying on of hands should be performed solemnly in silence; it is not just a hurried touching of the sick person's head. In making this gesture, we should imitate the solemnity of the imposition of hands at ordination.

Finally, let us mention briefly Viaticum, the sacrament of the dying, which we are all obliged to receive when the hour of our death approaches. In this important moment it is not anointing, but Viaticum, the Eucharist, that we need. Strengthened by the sacrament of anointing earlier in their illness, sick people can experience its effect throughout the whole of their illness. Then, strengthened by it, they are better prepared to imitate the death of Christ. The Church would like us to receive the Holy Viaticum under both species during the celebration of the Eucharist. To promote this, the Church not only permits but also recommends that, according to the circumstances, the Eucharist be celebrated near the sick-bed, with the family participating.

Chapter 14

THE LITURGY OF MARRIAGE

Marriage is both a secular institution and a sacrament, a sacred sign of an invisible reality. Even as a secular institution, marriage has its own sacred character since it arises from the Creator's will and therefore it could be considered a "natural sacrament" (*sacramentum naturae*). Because of the responsibility that it carries within itself, the preparation for marriage is very important from the natural point of view, and more so from the sacramental perspective. Already in the Old Testament, God had chosen the secular reality of the loving union of a man and woman to symbolize the divine love for Israel, and, in the New Testament, the love of Christ for his Church. Thus, the mutual love of couples becomes a visible sign of God's invisible love. On the other hand, God's love appears as the prototype and example for the couple's love.

The liturgical celebration of the sacrament of marriage developed gradually and became universal only in the second thousand years. In the second century Tertullian wrote: "How shall we describe the happiness of marriage, which the Church arranges, the oblation strengthens, upon which the blessing sets a seal, in which the angels are present as witnesses, and to which the Father gives his consent?" The first Christians were supposed to marry "according to the Lord," and their marriage was "made in the Lord," but the liturgical rite was rather minimal. Like others, Christians married according to Roman civil law by exchanging the consent between the bride and the groom. (It is interesting to note, that the question was posed to them in this way: "Do you want to be a mother or father of a family?" *Visne materfamilias [paterfamilias] esse?)* In the beginning, the Church's only participation seems to have been a blessing pronounced by the bishop at the wedding banquet. It was also a Roman custom to cover the bride with an amber veil, which was then extended over the groom's shoulder. Soon the couple began to participate in the nuptial Mass, during which the nuptial blessing was given. This became the most liturgical part of the ritual, which took over many elements of the secular wedding customs such as the exchange of rings and the joining of hands, tied by a stole and blessed by the priest. The nuptial blessing, a solemn form of prayer in the style of a *berakah*, blessed God, gave thanks and asked for his future presence in the couple's life *(epiklesis)*. In the Eastern Churches, the priest's blessing constitutes the essence of the sacrament and the priest is the minister; in the West the couple themselves are the ministers and the essence consists in the mutual exchange of consent. The East includes another symbol, the crowning *(stephanoma)* of the bride and groom.

There is no question that the mutual consent, that is, the mutual commitment to one another, is the legal and canonical requirement of the marriage rite. Legally it is a contract, although today it is looked upon much more as a covenant of love, exemplified in the LORD's covenant with Israel, and in the love-relationship between Christ, the bridegroom, and his bride, the Church. With the commitment of their lives, the couple also consents to undergo paschal transformation, that is, to die to themselves and begin to live for others, for their husband or wife. This death and resurrection can only be realized in Christ. Marriage conveys sanctifying grace, which again can be best seen in relationship to the three divine persons. The couple fulfils the Father's plan, which he kept in his heart from eternity for these two people and gradually brought them together in history. They are doing the Father's will when they join their lives together in the school of love that is marriage. Christ is often pictured as a *connuba*, the one who arranges the marriage. Couples must make Christ's love for his church present in their lives, to elevate their mutual human love to the supernatural level, so that each time they manifest to each other their love through sensible signs, they also communicate God's grace to each other and to others. By their love, Christian couples form the family or domestic church where they, husband and wife, become "priests" spreading that love to their children, their extended family and outsiders. Love thus becomes the cohesive force of the Church. The power of the Holy Spirit supports and helps their union, giving to their marital union a quasi-permanent character, where fidelity and exclusiveness reign. Thus, married couples form a special class within the Church, providing the church with successive generations and a school of love.

Among the dimensions of Christian marriage, we note the theological dimension, the revelation of God who is love. The christological dimension is clear in that spouses manifest the love of Christ to the Church through their mutual love. The Holy Spirit, enables couples to sacrifice for each other and for their children, and so die to themselves in order to live for Christ and for others. Herein lies the pneumatological dimension. The ecclesial dimension of marriage is shown in the formation of the domestic church in their family. Here they also foreshadow the eschatological banquet of the heavenly wedding feast, where all are united with Christ the Lamb.

Because of the lofty ideal and serious, though joyful, obligations that couples assume, it is imperative that the Christian community accompany them on their journey after the wedding. The Church should stand by them and help them in good times and bad. Couples should remember that their wedding rite is a source of grace for the rest of their lives; therefore they should renew their marriage vows on their anniversaries.

We mentioned above that veiling the bride was one of the Roman marriage customs. In this connection it is interesting to note that the same veiling had also been used among Christians for the consecration or veiling of virgins *(velatio virginum)*. This can often be found painted on the frescos of the catacombs. Obviously, the similarity is clear: the consecrated virgin is married to the Lord. This ancient, biblical concept of mystical marriage has been applied to those who have been chosen and have dedicated themselves completely to the Lord. Unfortunately today, this bridal mysticism has been largely abandoned, though it still has validity for anyone, male or female, who wants to serve the Lord alone, because they have fallen in love with him.

Chapter 15

THE LITURGY OF ORDINATION

We have seen already that all baptized Christians share Christ's priesthood. The apostolic ministry, that is, the successors of the apostles who were commissioned to continue the work of *kerygma, liturgia,* and *diakonia,* and to build up communities in the *koinonia* to share in it in a special way. We mentioned the essential and constitutional role of the ordained ministry of the Church when we spoke about the ecclesial dimension of the liturgy. This apostolic ministry is transmitted by the sacrament of ordination or holy orders. Holy orders include three degrees: episcopate, presbyterate, and diaconate, but here we will focus specifically on the ordination to the presbyterate. At one time the so-called minor orders were also treated under the heading of ordination because their conferral had some similarities with sacred orders. Now, instead of speaking of minor orders we speak of different ministries. Some are liturgical ministries such as acolytes and lectors, into which people are no longer ordained. Rather they are installed in a ministry.

The liturgy of ordination has the same characteristics as any other liturgy. Ordination happens during the Eucharistic celebration, and consists traditionally and essentially of the imposition of hands by the bishop upon the candidate's head, and in the consecratory, epicletic prayer. This, the most ancient part of the rite, is already indicated in the New Testament. The imposition of hands signifies both the transmission of an office, and the gift of the Holy Spirit. The consecratory prayer blesses *(berakah)* and thanks God for his plan of giving us leaders, and then pleads insistently *(epiklesis)* that the Holy Spirit come upon the candidate. Thus the rite symbolizes both the connection with the apostles through the laying on of hands and also the descent of the Holy Spirit.

The rite normally begins by calling the candidates by name *(vocatio),* symbolizing God's inner call directed to the individual, which the Church now communicates and expresses to him. The candidate's response: "Present," is not just an answer in a roll call, but a commitment. The Latin *Adsum* expresses it better: I am here, I am ready and willing to do your will! After the bishop's instruction about the office of priesthood, the candidate is asked about his willingness to assume the responsibilities of this office *(scrutinies)*. Then the candidate prostrates himself on the floor, and the whole community kneels to ask the intercession of the whole Church, including all the Saints, for this person to be ordained. The imposition of hands by the bishop and then by all the priests takes place in silence, as the assembly prays in the depths of their hearts for the Holy Spirit who is now conferred on the candidate in a special way. The consecratory prayer that follows includes the *epiklesis*. In this way the person officially becomes an ordained priest. Other rites further explain the office of presbyter: he is invested with the stole and chasuble, signs of his priestly ministry: he receives the chalice and paten with which he will offer the sacrifice of the Eucharist, and he is admonished to imitate what he is doing *(Imitamini quod tractatis)*,that is, to live the paschal mystery that he ritually celebrates in the Mass. His hands are anointed with sacred chrism, so that what he blesses may become truly blessed for the service and praise of God. Then the newly ordained priest concelebrates with the bishop, pronouncing for the first time the words of consecration "in the person of Christ" *(in persona Christi)*. After Mass or after his first Mass, he may give his first priestly blessing with his consecrated hands.

The sacrament of ordination first of all inserts the candidate into the order of the apostolic ministry by sealing him with the indelible sacramental character. On the basis of this, the person can perform actions proper to his office. Then he also receives an increase of sanctifying grace that can again be viewed in its different dimensions. Its theological dimension is the revelation of God's constant, challenging invitation to the world, whereby the priest becomes a permanent place of encounter between God and the human person.

Christologically, the priest is configured to Christ the high priest and head of the mystical body, becoming someone who personally makes Christ present throughout his whole life. The pneumatological dimension is realized when the Holy Spirit fills all the hidden corners of his heart and makes him an instrument of God's grace, changing him so that his whole being becomes a priest. Ecclesiologically, the priest manifests the Church as a structured community, a symbol that reminds the Church of its relationship to the historical Jesus. But most of all, the priest symbolizes Christ the head of the Church in relationship to the body of which he remains a member. From an anthropological viewpoint, the priest becomes from the moment of his ordination a "man for others," which means that he should gradually forget about himself to let Christ shine through his life for the sake of the world.

The marvellous moment of ordination of course remains a source of grace for the whole life of the priest. He ought to recall it (through *anamnesis!*) often: at the Chrism Mass when he renews his priestly vows, and on the anniversary of his ordination. It is an opportunity to "stir into flame the gift of God" which was given to him through the imposition of hands.

Appendix

SOME FORGOTTEN TRUTHS ABOUT THE PRIESTHOOD

(Homily at Vespers on the day of the Renewal of our Priestly Vows)

Tonight, at the Mass of Holy Chrism, the bishop will ask us to renew our commitment to the priesthood. This renewal of commitment happens in the context of the paschal mystery, just as the renewal of our baptismal commitment happens at the Easter Vigil. Both the mystery of baptism and the mystery of priesthood are closely connected with the Lord's paschal mystery.

The rite of renewal is simple: it consists of a few questions and answers. But in reality it is a grace event, a new encounter with the Lord. Christian theology assures us of the possibility of the revival of grace (*reviviscentia gratiae*), here in particular on the basis of the sacramental character of ordination. Therefore it is more than just answering a few questions. Following St. Paul's exhortation we want to stir up again the fire of the Holy Spirit, given to us through the imposition of hands. We want to return once again to that first love and enthusiasm for the Lord and his Church which we had on the day of our ordination. We want to re-experience that joyous moment when he called us, not just his servants but also his friends.

What should we do in order to experience anew the grace of ordination? We ought to open our hearts at least as much as on that day, answering and reaffirming the call with great generosity (*cum magno animo et cum magna liberalitate*): "Here I am, Lord, I am ready and willing to do your will!" Our "yes" ought to include all those things to which we committed ourselves: to become constructive members of the order of presbyters; to respect and obey the bishop by becoming his conscientious fellow-workers in caring for the flock of the Lord; to celebrate the mysteries, especially the Eucharist, with fidelity and devotion; to preach the Good News and to teach the Christian faith to all people with conviction and zeal; to consecrate (sacrifice, surrender) our life to God for the salvation of the people; and, finally, to unite ourselves every day more closely to Christ the High Priest. In return for this commitment we were filled with the Spirit of holiness that has changed our lives completely. It may therefore be useful to recall and reflect on some forgotten truths of the inexhaustible mystery of our priesthood.

1. *Insertion into the order of apostolic ministry*

The first result of ordination is that through the sacramental character we became members of the order of presbyters. "Order" is not so much an individual gift, but a collective term. We do not receive the order, but become members of this order, members of a group of people specially selected by the Lord to continue his work, the work of the apostles.

As a sacred order—hierarchy—this order is a constitutional element of the Church. To be sure, the Church is not just the hierarchy; the hierarchy in itself is only a skeleton. The body of Christ is a living organism, flesh and bones. Without flesh the Church remains a skeleton, but without a skeleton the Church is no more than an invertebrate mollusk.

By the nature of their ordination, priests cannot be isolated individuals. Essentially, they are members of the presbyteral order, the presbyter college, which exists to share the bishop's burden, to assist him and collaborate with him. Thus they form the *koinonia*, one of the deepest qualities of the Church, rediscovered at Vatican II. *Koinonia* means the faithful united with their priests and bishop around the eucharistic table. If this is true of all the faithful, all the more must it characterize the presbyterium! By their ordination they belong to this communal, collegial order, so that their lives and function must be always seen in this context of solidarity with one another. The Church cannot have *sacerdotes vagabundi*. Solidarity within this presbyteral order means friendship in good times and bad; sharing each other's burdens and being ready to help one another physically, spiritually, pastorally; responsibility *in solidum* for the local church, for the diocese, just as the bishop is responsible with pastoral solicitude for the well-being of the whole world-wide Church. Being a member of this Order also means growing together in love with our bishop and the Holy Father. It means loving the presbyterium, with all its faults and human features. It means being proud of being a member of it, proud of its 2000-year history, proud of its members in your own diocese and country, and even in the whole world.

2. Apostolicity of our Ministry

We believe in the apostolicity of the Church, which usually is described as apostolicity of doctrine and apostolicity of office. The apostolicity of doctrine means remaining faithful to the teaching of the apostles and includes the zealous effort to spread that teaching and translate it to people today. Though the whole Church is responsible to preserve and spread the Gospel, the Lord has chosen his apostles and their successors to guarantee this fidelity and apostolic zeal, and so he sent them into the world with this special commission.

Therefore the apostolic office exists for the sake of the apostolic doctrine. Because we know that Christianity is not just a doctrine, but a way of life, we have to say that besides the apostolic doctrine and the apostolic office we must preserve intact the apostolic lifestyle. The apostolic lifestyle means to live as the apostles lived. It means to always be a disciple who listens constantly to the Lord, sits at his feet, spends time with him, learns from him the secret and meaning of life, of his life and our lives which is the paschal mystery. We learn from him and then we try to put it into practice: how to do the Father's will rather than our own; how to suffer and die, but also how to rise to life; how to die to ourselves and live only for God and for others; how to be buried in the ground like the seed in order to bring a rich harvest; how to lose our life in order to gain it; how to be confident and hopeful in the midst of confusion and despair; how to cope with darkness and change it into light; how to change defeat into victory; how to transform even sin into the outpouring of God's love and mercy; how to be joyful and realistically optimistic in today's world because the Lord has said: "Trust in me! I have conquered the world. The victory is mine!"; how to look into the future with hope because the Lord is risen and therefore the future is bright.

The apostles had to learn this central mystery, the apostolic lifestyle, from the Lord himself. It was not easy for them. They were able to put it into practice only after the Holy Spirit filled their hearts. Then they were able to endure and rejoice in persecution because they had been found worthy to imitate their master and participate in his paschal mystery.

Such an apostolic lifestyle, living the paschal mystery, is the best and most important instrument of our apostolic ministry. Our ordained priesthood exists first of all and primarily to preach it, to teach the People of God to live out their baptismal commitment, to die and rise with Christ. Our own lifestyle must be a model for them. After our preaching and teaching, after giving example, our ordained priesthood then also enables them, through the sacraments and especially through the Eucharistic celebration, to join their own life and sacrifices to that of the Lord in his paschal transformation. I believe that only in this way can we be authentic priests of the Lord; only in this way will we be able to fulfill our mission to help the people "have life and have it more abundantly."

In the context of apostolicity, we should also remember briefly the question of apostolic succession. I am referring here to our responsibility for succession in the apostolic ministry. If we believe the constitutional necessity of this ministry for the Church, then I have to feel responsible that "other approved men" will follow after me. I cannot say; "*après moi le déluge!*" The priesthood has to continue, even if we have a whole range of lay ministries, as we should. It is true that the Lord is the one who calls, and gives the vocation, but I have to voice the Lord's challenge to young people. My voice and my lifestyle should attract followers, shouting into the world plainly and clearly: no other life is as meaningful and fulfilling as mine! If we just could manifest that "exceeding joy" (*aggalliasis*) which the early Christians experienced, we would not have to worry about the shortage of vocations to priesthood and religious life.

3. The Grace of Our Priesthood

At ordination we became members of the presbyteral order, participants in the apostolic ministry. Most of all, we were given the Holy Spirit anew with sacramental grace. The ancient ordination prayers talk about a special grace in each of the three degrees: deacons are given the "Spirit of zeal and service," bishops receive the "Spirit of leadership," and presbyters are filled with the "Spirit of Holiness" (*Pneuma tou hagiasmou*). In other words, the ancient church was conscious that priests must be holy; they are not just filling an office, but their status is the state of holiness.

Why do the Lord and the Church demand from priests this subjective (not only objective) holiness? Because no one can fulfill this office authentically unless he is holy or at least earnestly striving for holiness. It is a question of being credible. A priest must not just believe like other Christians. He must stand up and proclaim his faith, share his faith with others in a convincing way. Without this special grace, without this "spirit of holiness" kept alive in ourselves, priests simply cannot spend their entire lives being men of God, men of prayer, men for others who are always ready to go after the lost sheep, always kind and patient.

Priestly holiness consists in pastoral zeal, in being a good shepherd who is ready to lay down his life for the sheep. Priestly holiness is not contemplative, though we must be able to learn to see things with God's eyes – that is, become contemplatives in action. Priestly holiness is not cloistered, though we must find time for solitude, for just being with the Lord. Priestly holiness is active and apostolic holiness, so that even in our prayers we carry on the *sollicitudo* for our people and the Church.

This grace, the Spirit of holiness given us at the ordination, remains in us as the fountain of grace (*fons gratiae*) from which we can draw refreshing water at all times, but especially in times of discouragement (as today: because of the shortage of vocations, or the much-publicized low morale of priests, or some scandals), or when we feel overwhelmed by our inadequacy before the enormous task of our ministry. When we see traditional Christian values eroded, when crime is rampant, when people do not listen, when we are confused about right and wrong, then it is good to remember: "I am not Divine Providence." I am just a useless servant, weak and sinful. I am not going to redeem the world, but the Lord will. He called me, in spite of my sinfulness and inadequacy, to work for him and with him. Though he knew my past, my present and my future, he still wanted me as his friend and instrument. He decided to choose the weak to shame the strong of the world, and through our mumbling and fumbling he wanted to save the world!

4. Priesthood is a Personal Service to the Lord

Priesthood is not a community service, a paid job, or a comfortable nest. Priesthood is primarily and before anything else a personal service to the Lord himself. It is a call to friendship, intimacy, familiarity with him. This is why priests are not set up or appointed by the people on the basis of their qualifications, but chosen by the Lord according to his mysterious plan which selects the weak.

The Lord calls us to himself, above all to be his disciples, sitting at his feet, learning by personal encounter with him how to think, act, behave, love, shed tears, rejoice. He calls us to listen to his words, to his heart-beat (like John), and he teaches us the secret of life and of history: the paschal mystery.

Then, and only then, after spending time with him, he sends us on a mission: making him present everywhere and to everyone as his apostles and ambassadors; preaching the Good News that God is Love, that forgiveness is possible, that the future is bright, because he came not to condemn the world but to save it. In this enormous enterprise of transforming the world with the power of love, he is always with us to the end of the world. I am never alone. I am doing his work, not my own. It really doesn't matter whether I am successful or not, whether I see the result of my work or not; often others reap where we have sown. It does not matter if we are misunderstood, ridiculed, maltreated and persecuted; he was too, and disciples should be no different from their master. It doesn't even matter if we die on the cross; he did it before us, showing us the only way to save the world.

As a servant and friend of the Lord, I want to say and pray with the antiphon of today's Vespers: Place me at your side! (*Pone me juxta te*). Because if I am beside you, I am beside the fire. (*Qui juxta me est, juxta ignem est*). If I am beside you, I have no fear, and I can be whatever you want me to be.

5. Conclusion

In conclusion, let us recall the words from the Epistle to the Hebrews (12:1-13), which we read today in the Office of Readings: "And so, what of ourselves today? With all the witnesses of faith around us like a cloud," (with all the heroes of faith, past and present, especially among the prebyterium, even those here present), "let us also lay aside every weight and the sin that clings so closely," (and also every discouragement and temptation), "and let us run with perseverance the race that was set before us" (when we were ordained to the apostolic ministry), "looking to Jesus the pioneer and perfecter of our faith, who, for the sake of the joy that was set before him, endured the cross, disregarding its shame, and has taken his seat at the right hand of the throne of God."

Tonight, therefore, when we renew our commitment to the Lord, our answer should be generous: Out of love for Jesus and for his Church, we want to unite ourselves more closely to Jesus Christ and try to be like him. We want to be faithful ministers of his mysteries. And we want to keep our eyes always fixed on Jesus! Amen.

AGMV Marquis
MEMBER OF SCABRINI MEDIA
Quebec, Canada
2001